T0222521

Modern Programming Made Easy

Using Java, Scala, Groovy, and JavaScript

Second Edition

Adam L. Davis

Apress®

Modern Programming Made Easy: Using Java, Scala, Groovy, and JavaScript

Adam L. Davis
Oviedo, FL, USA

ISBN-13 (pbk): 978-1-4842-5568-1   ISBN-13 (electronic): 978-1-4842-5569-8
https://doi.org/10.1007/978-1-4842-5569-8

Managing Director, Apress Media LLC: Welmoed Spahr
Acquisitions Editor: Steve Anglin
Development Editor: Matthew Moodie
Coordinating Editor: Mark Powers

Cover designed by eStudioCalamar

Cover image designed by Freepik (www.freepik.com)

Distributed to the book trade worldwide by Springer Science+Business Media, 1 New York Plaza, New York, NY 10004, U.S.A.. Phone 1-800-SPRINGER, fax (201) 348-4505, e-mail orders-ny@ springer-sbm.com, or visit www.springeronline.com. Apress Media, LLC is a California LLC and the sole member (owner) is Springer Science + Business Media Finance Inc (SSBM Finance Inc). SSBM Finance Inc is a **Delaware** corporation.

For information on translations, please e-mail editorial@apress.com; for reprint, paperback, or audio rights, please email bookpermissions@springernature.com.

Apress titles may be purchased in bulk for academic, corporate, or promotional use. eBook versions and licenses are also available for most titles. For more information, reference our Print and eBook Bulk Sales web page at http://www.apress.com/bulk-sales.

Any source code or other supplementary material referenced by the author in this book is available to readers on GitHub via the book's product page, located at www.apress.com/9781484255681. For more detailed information, please visit http://www.apress.com/source-code.

Printed on acid-free paper

Dedicated to all teachers.
Thank you for teaching!

Table of Contents

About the Author

Adam L. Davis makes software. He's spent many years developing in Java (since Java 1.2) and has enjoyed using Spring and Hibernate for more than a decade. Since 2006 he's been using Groovy, Grails, HTML, CSS, and JavaScript, in addition to Java, to create SaaS web applications that help track finances for large institutions (among other things).

Adam has a master's and a bachelor's degree in Computer Science from Georgia Tech. He is also the author of *Reactive Streams in Java* (Apress, 2019) and *Learning Groovy 3, Second Edition* (Apress, 2019). You can check out his web site at `https://github.adamldavis.com/`.

About the Technical Reviewer

Manuel Jordan Elera is an autodidactic developer and researcher who enjoys learning new technologies for his own experiments and creating new integrations. Manuel won the Springy Award—Community Champion and Spring Champion 2013. In his little free time, he reads the Bible and composes music on his guitar. Manuel is known as dr_pompeii. He has tech-reviewed numerous books for Apress, including *Pro Spring Boot 2* (2019), *Rapid Java Persistence and Microservices* (2019), *Java Language Features* (2018), *Spring Boot 2 Recipes* (2018), and *Java APIs, Extensions and Librarie*s (2018). Read his 13 detailed tutorials about many Spring technologies, contact him through his blog at www.manueljordanelera.blogspot.com, and follow him on his Twitter account, @dr_pompeii.

CHAPTER 1

Introduction

In my experience, learning how to program (in typical computer science classes) can be very difficult. The curriculum tends to be boring, abstract, and unattached to "real-world" coding. Owing to how fast technology progresses, computer science classes tend to teach material that is very quickly out of date and out of touch. I believe that teaching programming could be much simpler, and I hope this book achieves that goal.

Note There's going to be a lot of tongue-in-cheek humor throughout this book, but this first part is serious. Don't worry, it gets better.

Problem-Solving

Before you learn to program, the task can seem rather daunting, much like looking at a mountain before you climb it. However, over time, you will realize that programming is really about problem-solving.

On your journey toward learning to code, as with so much in life, you will encounter many obstacles. You may have heard it before, but it really is true: the path to success is to try, try, and try again. People who persevere the most tend to be the most successful people.

© Adam L. Davis 2020
A. L. Davis, *Modern Programming Made Easy*,
https://doi.org/10.1007/978-1-4842-5569-8_1

Programming is fraught with trial and error. Although things will get easier over time, you'll never be right all the time. So, much as with most things in life, you must be patient, diligent, and curious to be successful.

About This Book

This book is organized into several chapters, beginning with the most basic concepts. If you already understand a concept, you can safely move ahead to the next chapter. Although this book concentrates on Java, it also refers to other languages, such as Groovy, Scala, and JavaScript, so you will gain a deeper understanding of concepts common to all programming languages.

Tips   Text styled like this provides additional information that you may find helpful.

Info   Text styled this way usually refers the curious reader to additional information.

Warnings   Text such as this cautions the wary reader. Many have fallen along the path of computer programming.

Exercises   This is an exercise. We learn best by doing, so it's important that you try these out.

CHAPTER 2

Software to Install

Before you begin to program, you must install some basic tools.

Java/Groovy

For Java and Groovy, you will have to install the following:

- JDK (Java Development Kit), such as OpenJDK 11. You can install OpenJDK by following the instructions at adoptopenjdk.net.[1]

- IDE (Integrated Development Environment), such as NetBeans 11.

- *Groovy*: A dynamic language similar to Java that runs on the JVM (Java Virtual Machine).

---

[1]https://adoptopenjdk.net/installation.html

© Adam L. Davis 2020
A. L. Davis, *Modern Programming Made Easy*,
https://doi.org/10.1007/978-1-4842-5569-8_2

✎ Install Java and NetBeans 11 or higher. Download and install the Java JDK and NetBeans.[2] Open NetBeans and select File ➤ New Project… ➤ Java with Gradle, Java Application. When asked, provide the group "test," version "0.1," and package such as "com. gradleproject1". Click "Finish," then "OK."

Install Groovy: Go to the Groovy web site and install Groovy.[3]

Trying It Out

After installing Groovy, you should use it to try coding. Open a command prompt (or terminal), type groovyConsole, and hit Enter to begin.

✎ In groovyConsole, type the following and then hit Ctrl+r to run the code.

1   print "hello"

Because most Java code is valid Groovy code, you should keep the Groovy console open and use it to try out all of the examples from this book.

You can also easily try out JavaScript in the following way:

- Just open your web browser and go to jsfiddle.net.

---

[2]https://netbeans.apache.org/download/index.html
[3]https://groovy.apache.org/download.html

Others

Once you have the preceding installed, you should eventually install the following:

- *Scala*[4]: An object-oriented language built on the JVM

- *Git*[5]: A version control program

- *Maven*[6]: A modular build tool

Go ahead and install these, if you're in the mood. I'll wait.

To try out Scala, type `scala` in your command prompt or terminal once you have installed it.

Code on GitHub

A lot of the code from this book is available on `github.com/modernprog`.[7] You can go there at any time to follow along with the book.

---

[4]`www.scala-lang.org/`
[5]`https://git-scm.com/`
[6]`https://maven.apache.org/`
[7]`https://github.com/modernprog`

CHAPTER 3

The Basics

In this chapter, we'll cover the basic syntax of Java and similar languages.

Coding Terms

Source file refers to human-readable code. *Binary file* refers to computer-readable code (the compiled code). In Java, this binary code is called *bytecode* which is read by the *Java Virtual Machine (JVM)*.

In Java, the source files end with `.java`, and binary files end with `.class` (also called class files). You *compile* source files using a *compiler,* which gives you binary files or bytecode.

In Java, the compiler is called `javac`; in Groovy it is `groovyc`; and it is `scalac` in Scala (see a trend here?). All three of these languages can be compiled to bytecode and run on the JVM. The bytecode is a common format regardless of which programming language it was generated from.

However, some languages, such as JavaScript, don't have to be compiled. These are called *interpreted languages*. JavaScript can run in your browser (such as Firefox or Google Chrome), or it can run on a server using *Node.js*, a JavaScript runtime built on Chrome's V8 JavaScript engine.

© Adam L. Davis 2020
A. L. Davis, *Modern Programming Made Easy*,
https://doi.org/10.1007/978-1-4842-5569-8_3

Primitives and Reference

Primitive types in Java refer to different ways to store numbers and have practical significance. The following primitives exist in Java:

- `char`: A single character, such as A (the letter *A*).

- `byte`: A number from -128 to 127 (8 bits[1]). Typically, a way to store or transmit raw data.

- `short`: A 16 bits signed integer. It has a maximum of about 32,000.

- `int`: A 32 bits signed integer. Its maximum is about 2 to the 31st power.

- `long`: A 64 bits signed integer. Maximum of 2 to the 63rd power.

- `float`: A 32 bits floating-point number. This format stores fractions in base two and does not translate directly to base ten numbers (how numbers are usually written). It can be used for things such as simulations.

- `double`: Like `float` but with 64 bits.

- `boolean`: Has only two possible values: `true` and `false` (much like 1 bit).

 See Java Tutorial—Data Types[2] for more information.

---

[1] A bit is the smallest possible amount of information. It corresponds to a 1 or 0.
[2] https://docs.oracle.com/javase/tutorial/java/nutsandbolts/datatypes.html

GROOVY, SCALA, AND JAVASCRIPT

Groovy types are much the same as Java's. In Scala, everything is an object, so primitives don't exist. However, they are replaced with corresponding *value types* (Int, Long, etc.). JavaScript has only one type of number, Number, which is similar to Java's float.

A *variable* is a value in memory referred to by a name. In Java you can declare a variable as a primitive by writing the type then any valid name. For example, to create an integer named price with an initial value of 100, write the following:

```
1   int price = 100;
```

Every other type of variable in Java is a *reference*. It points to some object in memory. This will be covered later on.

In Java, each primitive type also has a corresponding class type: Byte for byte, Integer for int, Long for long, and so on. Using the class type allows the variable to be null (meaning no value). However, using the primitive type can have better performance when handling a lot of values. Java can automatically wrap and unwrap primitives in their corresponding classes (this is called *boxing* and *unboxing*).

Strings/Declarations

A S*tring* is a list of characters (text). It is a very useful built-in class in Java (and most languages). To define a string, you simply surround some text in quotes. For example:

```
1   String hello = "Hello World!";
```

Here the variable hello is assigned the string "Hello World!".

In Java, you must put the type of the variable in the declaration. That's why the first word here is String.

In Groovy and JavaScript, strings can also be surrounded by single quotes ('hello'). Also, declaring variables is different in each language. Groovy allows you to use the keyword def, while JavaScript and Scala use var. Java 10 also introduced using var to define local variables. For example:

```
1   def hello = "Hello Groovy!" //groovy
2   var hello = "Hello Scala/JS!" //Scala or JS
```

Statements

Almost every statement in Java must end in a semicolon (;). In many other languages, such as Scala, Groovy, and JavaScript, the semicolon is optional, but in Java, it is necessary. Much as how periods at the end of each sentence help you to understand the written word, the semicolon helps the compiler understand the code.

By convention, we usually put each statement on its own line, but this is not required, as long as semicolons are used to separate each statement.

Assignment

Assignment is an extremely important concept to understand, but it can be difficult for beginners. However, once you understand it, you will forget how hard it was to learn.

Let's start with a metaphor. Imagine you want to hide something valuable, such as a gold coin. You put it in a safe place and write the address on a piece of paper. This paper is like a reference to the gold. You can pass it around and even make copies of it, but the gold remains in the same place and does not get copied. On the other hand, anyone with the reference to the gold can get to it. This is how a *reference variable* works.

Let's look at an example:

```
1   String gold = "Au";
2   String a = gold;
3   String b = a;
4   b = "Br";
```

After running the preceding code, gold and a refer to the string "Au", while b refers to "Br".

Class and Object

A *class* is the basic building block of code in object-oriented languages. A class typically defines state and behavior. The following class is named SmallClass:

```
1   package com.example.mpme;
2   public class  SmallClass  {
3   }
```

Class names always begin with an uppercase letter in Java. It's common practice to use CamelCase to construct the names. This means that instead of using spaces (or anything else) to separate words, we uppercase the first letter of each word.

The first line is the package of the class. A package is like a directory on the file system. In fact, in Java, the package must actually match the path to the Java source file. So, the preceding class would be located in the path com/example/mpme/ in the source file system. Packages help to organize code and allow multiple classes to have the same name as long as they are in different packages.

An *object* is an instance of a class in memory. Because a class can have multiple values within it, an instance of a class will store those values.

✏️ Create a Class

- Open your IDE (NetBeans).

- Note the common organizational structure of a typical Java project in the file system:

  - `src/main/java`: Java classes

  - `src/main/resources`: Non-Java resources

  - `src/test/java`: Java test classes

  - `src/test/resources`: Non-Java test resources

- Right-click your Java project and choose New ➤ Java Class. Under "Class-Name" put "SmallClass". Put "com.example.mpme" for the package name.

Fields, Properties, and Methods

Next you might want to add some properties and methods to your class. A *field* is a value associated with a particular value or object. A *property* is essentially a field which has a "getter" or "setter" or both (a *getter* gets the value and a *setter* sets the value of a property). A *method* is a block of code on a class which can be called later on (it doesn't do anything until called).

```
1   package  com.example.mpme;
2   public  class  SmallClass  {
3       String name; //field
4       String getName() {return  name;} //getter
5       void print() {System.out.println(name);} //method
6   }
```

In the preceding code, name is a property, getName is a special method called a getter, and print is a method which does not return anything (this is what void means). Here, name is defined to be a String. System.out is built into the JDK and links to "standard out" which we discuss later, and println prints text and appends a newline to the output.

Methods can have parameters (values passed into the method), modify fields of the class, and can have return values (a value returned by the method) using the return statement. For example, modify the preceding method, print, to the following:

```
1   public String print(String value) {
2       name = "you gave me " + value;
3       System.out.println(name);
4       return name;
5   }
```

This method changes the name field, prints out the new value, and then returns that value. Try this new method out in the groovyConsole by defining the class and then executing the following:

```
1   new SmallClass().print("you gave me dragons")
```

Groovy Classes

Groovy is extremely similar to Java but always defaults to public (we will cover what public means in a later chapter).

```
1   package com.example.mpme;
2   class SmallClass {
3       String name //property
4       def print() { println(name) } //method
5   }
```

Groovy also automatically gives you "getter" and "setter" methods for properties, so writing the getName method would have been redundant.

JavaScript Prototypes

Although JavaScript has objects, it doesn't have a class keyword (prior to ECMAScript 2015). Instead, it uses a concept called prototype. For example, creating a class can look like the following:

```
1   function SmallClass() {}
2   SmallClass.prototype.name = "name"
3   SmallClass.prototype.print = function() { console.log(this.
    name) }
```

Here name is a property and print is a method.

Scala Classes

Scala has a very concise syntax, which puts the properties of a class in parentheses. Also, types come after the name and a colon. For example:

```
1   class SmallClass(var name:String) {
2       def  print = println(name)
3   }
```

Creating a New Object

In all four languages, creating a new object uses the new keyword. For example:

```
1   sc = new  SmallClass();
```

Comments

As a human, it is sometimes useful for you to leave notes in your source code for other humans—and even for yourself, later. We call these notes *comments*. You write comments thus:

```
1   String gold = "Au"; // this is a comment
2   String a = gold; // a is now "Au"
3   String b = a; // b is now  "Au"
4   b = "Br";
5   /* b is now "Br".
6      this is still a comment */
```

Those last two lines demonstrate multiline comments. So, in summary:

- Two forward slashes denote the start of a single-line comment.

- Slash-asterisk marks the beginning of a multiline comment.

- Asterisk-slash marks the end of a multiline comment.

Comments are the same in all languages covered in this book.

Summary

In this chapter, you learned the basic concepts of programming:

- Compiling source files into binary files

- How objects are instances of classes

- Primitive types, references, and strings

- Fields, methods, and properties

- Variable assignment

- How source code comments work

CHAPTER 4

Math

(Or *Maths*, if you prefer.)

Adding, Subtracting, etc.

Your friend Bob was just bitten by a zombie but escaped alive. Unfortunately, there is now one more zombie to worry about.

```
1    zombies = zombies + 1;
```

There's a shorter way to write the same thing (and we are pressed for time here; the zombies are coming).

```
1    zombies += 1;
```

Actually, there's an even shorter way to write this, and it's called the *increment operator*.

```
1    zombies++;
```

Luckily, there's also a *decrement operator* (to use when we kill a zombie).

```
1    zombie--;
```

© Adam L. Davis 2020
A. L. Davis, *Modern Programming Made Easy*,
https://doi.org/10.1007/978-1-4842-5569-8_4

Adding and subtracting are easy enough, but what about their cousins, multiplying and dividing? Luckily these symbols are the same in virtually every programming language: ∗ and /.

```
1    int legs = zombies * 2;
2    int halfZombies = zombies / 2;
```

Numbers written in Java are of type int by default. But what if we want to deal with fractions that are not whole numbers?

```
1    float oneThirdZombies = zombies / 3.0f;
```

No, 3.0f is not a typo. The f makes 3 a float. You can use lower- or uppercase letters (D means double; F means float; and L means long).

This is where math starts to get tricky. To engage *float division* (remember from Chapter 3, float is an imprecise number), we need 3 to be a float. If we instead wrote zombies / 3, this would result in *integer division*, and the remainder would be lost. For example, 32 / 3 is 10.

MODULO

You don't really need to understand Modulo, but if you want to, keep reading. Imagine that you and three buddies want to attack a group of zombies. You have to know how many each of you has to kill, so that each of you kills an equal number of zombies. For this you do integer division.

```
1    int numberToKill = zombies / 4;
```

But you want to know how many will be left over. For this, you require *modulo* (%):

```
1    int leftOverZombies = zombies % 4;
```

This gives you the *remainder* of dividing zombies by four.

More Complex Math

If you want to do anything other than add, subtract, multiply, divide, and modulo, you will have to use the java.lang.Math class. The Math class is part of the *Java Development Kit (JDK)* which is always available as part of core Java. There are many such classes which we will encounter as we go.

Let's say you want to raise a number to the power of 2. For example, if you want to estimate the exponentially increasing number of zombies, as follows:

```
1    double nextYearEstimate = Math.pow(numberOfZombies, 2.0d);
```

This type of method is called a *static method since it does not require an object instance.* (Don't worry, you'll learn more about this later.) Here's a summary of the most commonly used methods in java.lang.Math.

- abs: Returns the absolute value of a value

- min: The minimum of two numbers

- max: The maximum of two numbers

- pow: Returns the value of the first argument raised to the power of the second argument

- sqrt: Returns the correctly rounded positive square root of a double value

- cos: Returns the trigonometric cosine of an angle

- sin: Returns the trigonometric sine of an angle

- tan: Returns the trigonometric tangent of an angle

ℹ For a list of all the methods in Math, see the Java docs.[1]

⚭ Sine   If you're unfamiliar with sine and cosine, they are very useful whenever you want to draw a circle, for example. If you're on your computer right now and want to learn more about sine and cosine, please look at this animation[2] referenced in the footnote at the end of this page and keep watching it until you understand the sine wave.

Random Numbers

The easiest way to create a random number is to use the Math.random() method.

The random() method returns a double value greater than or equal to zero and less than one.

For example, to simulate a roll of the dice (to determine who gets to deal with the next wave of zombies), use the following:

```
1   int roll = (int) (Math.random() * 6);
```

This would result in a random number from 0 to 5. We could then add one to get the numbers 1 to 6. We need to have (int) here to convert the double returned from random() to an int—this is called *casting*.

---

[1]https://docs.oracle.com/en/java/javase/11/docs/api/java.base/java/lang/Math.html

[2]https://upload.wikimedia.org/wikipedia/commons/0/08/Sine_curve_drawing_animation.gif

JavaScript also has a `Math.random()` method. For example, to get a random integer between `min` (included) and `max` (excluded), you would do the following (`Math.floor` returns the largest integer less than or equal to a given number):

```
1    Math.floor(Math.random() * (max - min)) + min;
```

However, if you want to create lots of random numbers in Java, it's better to use the `java.util.Random` class instead. It has several different methods for creating random numbers, including

- `nextInt(int n)`: A random number from 0 to n (not including n)

- `nextInt()`: A random number uniformly distributed across all possible `int` values

- `nextLong()`: Same as `nextInt()` but for `long`

- `nextFloat()`: Same as `nextInt()` but for `float`

- `nextDouble()`: Same as `nextInt()` but for `double`

- `nextBoolean()`: True or false

- `nextBytes(byte[] bytes)`: Fills the given byte array with random bytes

You must first create a new `Random` object, then you can use it to create random numbers, as follows:

```
1    Random randy = new Random();
2    int roll6 = randy.nextInt(6) + 1; // 1 to 6
3    int roll12 = randy.nextInt(12) + 1; // 1 to 12
```

Now you can create random numbers and do math with them. Hurray!

⚿ Seeds   If you create a Random with a seed (e.g., new Random(1234)), it will always generate the same sequence of random numbers when given the same seed.

Summary

In this chapter, you learned how to program math, such as

- How to add, subtract, multiply, divide, and modulo

- Using the Math library in Java

- Creating random numbers

CHAPTER 5

Arrays, Lists, Sets, and Maps

So far, I've only talked about single values, but in programming, you often have to work with large collections of values. For this, we have many data structures that are built into the language. These are similar for Java, Groovy, Scala, and even JavaScript.

Arrays

An *array* is a fixed size collection of data values.

You declare an array type in Java by appending [ ] to the type. For example, an array of ints is defined as int[ ].

```
1   int[] vampireAges = new int[10]; // ten vampires
```

Setting and accessing the values in an array uses the same square bracket syntax, such as the following:

```
1   vampireAges[0] = 1565; // set age of first vampire
2   int age = vampireAges[0]  // get age of first vampire
```

As you can see, the first index of an array is zero. Things tend to start at zero when programming; try to remember this.

© Adam L. Davis 2020
A. L. Davis, *Modern Programming Made Easy*,
https://doi.org/10.1007/978-1-4842-5569-8_5

Q Patient 0   Here's a helpful metaphor: the first person to start an outbreak (a zombie outbreak, for example) is known as patient zero, not patient one. Patient one is the *second* person infected.

This also means that the *last* index of the array is always one less than the size of the array. This is also true for lists.

```
1   vampireAges[9] = 442; // last vampire
```

You can reassign and access array values just like any other variable.

```
1   int year = 2020; // current year
2   int firstVampBornYear = year - vampireAges[0];
```

You can also declare arrays of objects as well. In this case, each element of the array is a reference to an object in memory. For example, the following would declare an array of Vampire objects:

```
1   Vampire[] vampires = new Vampire[10]; // Vampire array with
length 10
```

You can also populate your array directly, such as if you're creating an array of strings, for example.

```
1   String[] names = {"Dracula", "Edward"};
```

The Array object in JavaScript is more like a Java List. Java arrays are a somewhat low-level structure used only for performance reasons. In Groovy 3, the Java-style declaration of arrays is supported. In previous versions you would have to use the List style, which we cover next.

In Scala, you can define an Array like one of the following:

```
1   var names = new Array[String](2) // size of 2 without values
2   var names = Array("Dracula", "Edward") // size of 2 with values
```

Lists

Of course, we don't always know how many elements we need to store in an array. For this reason (and many others), programmers invented List, a re-sizable collection of ordered elements.

In Java, you create List<E> in the following way:

```
1   List<Vampire> vampires = new ArrayList<>();
```

The class between the first angle brackets (<>) defines the *generic type* of the list—what can go into the list (in this case it is Vampire). The second set of angle brackets can be empty since Java can infer the generic type from the left side of the expression. You can now add vampires to this list all day, and it will expand, as necessary in the background.

You add to List like this:

```
1   vampires.add(new  Vampire("Count Dracula", 1897));
```

List also contains tons of other useful methods, including

- size(): Gets the size of List
- get(int index): Gets the value at that index
- remove(int index): Removes the value at that index
- remove(Object o): Removes the given object
- isEmpty(): Returns true only if List is empty
- clear(): Removes all values from List

⚹ In Java, List is an interface (we'll cover interfaces in depth in Chapter 8) and has many different implementations, but here are two:

- java.util.ArrayList
- java.util.LinkedList

The only difference you should care about is that, in general, LinkedList grows faster when inserting a value at an arbitrary index, while ArrayList's get() method is faster at an arbitrary index.

You'll learn how to loop through lists, arrays, and sets (and what "loop" means) in the next chapter. For now, just know that lists are a fundamental concept in programming.

Groovy Lists

Groovy has a simpler syntax for creating lists, which is built into the language.

```
1   def list = []
2   list.add(new Vampire("Count Dracula", 1897))
3   // or
4   list << new Vampire("Count Dracula", 1897)
```

Scala Lists

In Scala, you create a list and add to a list in a slightly different way:

```
1   var list = List[Vampire]();
2   list :+ new Vampire("Count Dracula", 1897)
```

Also, this actually creates a new list, instead of modifying the existing list (it reuses the existing list in the background for performance reasons). This is because the default List in Scala is *immutable*, meaning it cannot be modified (the default implementation is immutable, but you can use a mutable implementation from the scala.collection.mutable package). Although this may seem strange, in conjunction with *functional* programming, it makes parallel programming (programming for multiple processors) easier as we'll see in Chapter 10.

JavaScript Arrays

As mentioned earlier, JavaScript uses Array[1] instead of List. Also, since JavaScript is not strictly typed, an Array can always hold objects of any type.

Arrays can be created much like lists in Groovy. However, the methods available are somewhat different. For example, push is used instead of add.

```
1   def array = []
2   array.push(new Vampire("Count Dracula", 1897))
```

You can also declare the initial values of Array. For example, the following two lines are equivalent:

```
1   def years = [1666, 1680, 1722]
2   def years = new Array(1666, 1680, 1722)
```

To add to the confusion, arrays in JavaScript can be accessed much like Java arrays. For example:

```
1   def firstYear = years[0]
2   def size = years.length
```

---

[1]https://developer.mozilla.org/en-US/docs/Web/JavaScript/Reference/Global_Objects/Array

Sets

Set<E> is much like List<E>, but each value or object can only have one instance in the Set, whereas in previous collections, there can be repeats.

Set has many of the same methods as List. However, it is missing the methods that use an index, because Set is not necessarily in any particular order.

```
1    Set<String> dragons = new HashSet<>();
2    dragons.add("Lambton");
3    dragons.add("Deerhurst");
4    dragons.size(); // 2
5    dragons.remove("Lambton");
6    dragons.size(); // 1
```

Note   To preserve insertion order, you can use a
LinkedHashSet<E> which uses a doubly linked list to store
the order of the elements in addition to a hash table to preserve
uniqueness.

In Java, there is such a thing as SortedSet<E>, which is implemented by TreeSet<E>. For example, let's say you wanted a sorted list of names, as follows:

```
1    SortedSet<String> dragons = new TreeSet<>();
2    dragons.add("Lambton");
3    dragons.add("Smaug");
4    dragons.add("Deerhurst");
5    dragons.add("Norbert");
6    System.out.println(dragons);
7    // [Deerhurst, Lambton, Norbert, Smaug]
```

TreeSet will magically always be sorted in the proper order.

Q Okay, it's not really magic. The object to be sorted must implement the Comparable interface, but you haven't learned about interfaces yet (interfaces are covered in Chapter 8).

JavaScript does not yet have a built-in Set class. Groovy uses the same classes for Set as Java. Scala has its own implementations of Set. For example, you can define a normal Set or SortedSet in Scala as follows:

```
1   var nums = Set(1, 2, 3)
2   var sortedNums = SortedSet(1, 3, 2)
```

Maps

Map<K,V> is a collection of keys associated with values. The K specifies the generic type for keys, and the V specifies the generic type for values. It may be easier to understand with an example:

```
1   Map<String,String> map = new  HashMap<>();
2   map.put("Smaug", "deadly");
3   map.put("Norbert", "cute");
4   map.size(); // 2
5   map.get("Smaug"); // deadly
```

Map also has the following methods:

- containsKey(Object key): Returns true, if this map contains a mapping for the specified key

- containsValue(Object value): Returns true, if this map maps one or more keys to the specified value

- keySet(): Returns a Set view of the keys contained in this map

- putAll(Map m): Copies all of the mappings from the specified map to this map

- remove(Object key): Removes the mapping for a key from this map, if it is present

Groovy Maps

Just as for List, Groovy has a simpler syntax for creating and editing Map.

```
1   def map = ["Smaug": "deadly"]
2   map.Norbert = "cute"
3   println(map) // [Smaug:deadly, Norbert:cute]
```

Scala Maps

Scala's Map syntax is also somewhat shorter.

```
1   var map = Map("Smaug" -> "deadly")
2   var  map2 =  map + ("Norbert" -> "cute")
3   println(map2) // Map(Smaug -> deadly, Norbert -> cute)
```

As with List and Set, Scala's default Map is also immutable.

JavaScript Maps

JavaScript does not yet have a built-in Map class, but it can be approximated by using the built-in Object[2] syntax. For example:

```
1   def map = {"Smaug": "deadly", "Norbert": "cute"}
```

---

[2]https://developer.mozilla.org/en-US/docs/Web/JavaScript/Reference/
Global_Objects/Object

You could then use either of the following to access map values: `map.Smaug` or `map["Smaug"]`.

Summary

This chapter introduced you to the following concepts:

- *Arrays*: Collections of data with a fixed size

- *Lists*: An expandable collection of objects or values

- *Sets*: An expandable collection of unique objects or values

- *Maps*: A dictionary-like collection

CHAPTER 6

Conditionals and Loops

To rise above the label of *calculator*, a programming language must have conditional statements and loops.

A *conditional statement* is a statement that may or may not execute, depending on the circumstances.

A *loop* is a statement that gets repeated multiple times.

If, Then, Else

The most basic conditional statement is the `if` statement. It executes some code only if a given condition is true. It is the same in all languages covered in this book. For example:

```
1   if (vampire) { // vampire is a boolean
2         useWoodenStake();
3   }
```

Curly brackets (`{}`) define a block of code (in Java, Scala, Groovy, and JavaScript). To define what should happen if your condition is `false`, you use the `else` keyword.

```
1   if (vampire) {
2         useWoodenStake();
```

© Adam L. Davis 2020

A. L. Davis, *Modern Programming Made Easy*,
https://doi.org/10.1007/978-1-4842-5569-8_6

```
3    } else {
4            useAxe();
5    }
```

Actually, this can be shortened, because in this case we only have one statement per condition.

```
1    if (vampire) useWoodenStake();
2    else useAxe();
```

It's generally better to use the curly bracket style in Java to avoid any accidents later on when another programmer adds more code. If you have multiple conditions you have to test, you can use the else if style, such as the following:

```
1    if  (vampire) useWoodenStake();
2    else if (zombie) useBat();
3    else useAxe();
```

Switch Statements

Sometimes you have so many conditions that your else if statements span several pages. In this case, you might consider using the switch keyword. It allows you to test for several different values of the same variable. For example:

```
1    switch (monsterType) {
2    case "Vampire": useWoodenStake(); break;
3    case "Zombie": useBat(); break;
4    case "Orc": shoutInsult();
5    default: useAxe();
6    }
```

The case keyword denotes the value to be matched.

The break keyword always causes the program to exit the current code block. This is necessary in a switch statement; otherwise, every statement after the case will be executed. For example, in the preceding code, when monsterType is "Orc", both shoutInsult and useAxe are executed because there is no break after shoutInsult().

The default keyword denotes the code to execute if none of the other cases are matched. It is much like the final else block of an if/else block.

⌕ There is more to switch statements, but this involves concepts we'll cover later on, so we'll return to this topic.

Figure 6-1. *Formal Logic—XKCD 1033 (courtesy* http://xkcd. com/1033/)

Boolean Logic

Computers use a special kind of math called *Boolean logic* (it's also called *Boolean algebra*). All you really need to know are the following three Boolean operators and six comparators. The operators first:

&& — AND: `true` only if left and right values are `true`

|| — OR: `true` if either left or right value is `true`

! — NOT: Negates a Boolean (`true` becomes `false`; `false` becomes `true`)

Now the comparators:

== — Equal: True if both values are equal.

!= — Not Equal: The left and right values are not equal.

< — Less than: The left side is less than the right.

> — Greater than: The left side is greater than the right.

<= — Less than or equal.

>= — Greater than or equal.

Conditions (such as `if`) operate on Boolean values (`true`/`false`)—the same boolean type that you learned about in Chapter 3. When used properly, all the preceding operators result in a Boolean value.

For example:

```
1   if (age > 120 && skin == Pale && !wrinkled) {
2           probablyVampire();
3   }
```

Looping

The two simplest ways to loop are the while loop and do/while loop.

The while loop simply repeats while the *loop condition* is true. The while condition is tested at the start of each run of the loop.

```
1    boolean repeat = true;
2    while (repeat) {
3            doSomething();
4            repeat = false;
5    }
```

The preceding would call the doSomething() method once. The loop condition in the preceding code is repeat. This is a simple example. Usually, the loop condition would be something more complex.

The do loop is like the while loop, except that it always goes through at least one time. The while condition is tested after each run through the loop. For example:

```
1    boolean repeat = false;
2    do  {
3            doSomething();
4    } while(repeat);
```

It's often helpful to increment a number in your loop, for example:

```
1    int i = 0;
2    while (i < 10) {
3            doSomething(i);
4            i++;
5    }
```

The preceding loop, which loops ten times, can be condensed using the for loop as follows:

```
1    for (int  i = 0; i < 10; i++) {
2              doSomething(i);
3    }
```

The for loop has an initiation clause, a loop condition, and an increment clause. The *initiation clause* comes first (int i = 0 in the preceding loop) and is only called once before the loop is run. The *loop condition* comes next (i < 10) and is much like a while condition. The *increment clause* comes last (i++) and is called after each loop execution. This style of loop is useful for looping through an array with an index. For example:

```
1    String[] strArray = {"a", "b", "c"};
2    for (int i = 0; i < strArray.length; i++)
3              System.out.print(strArray[i]);
```

This would print "abc." The preceding loop is equivalent to the following:

```
1    int i = 0;
2    while  (i < strArray.length) {
3         String str = strArray[i];
4              System.out.print(str);
5              i++;
6    }
```

In Java, you can write for loops in a more concise way for an array or collection (list or set). For example:

```
1    String[] strArray = {"a", "b", "c"};
2    for  (String str : strArray)
3              System.out.print(str);
```

This is called a for each loop. Note that it uses a colon instead of a semicolon.

Summary

In this chapter, you learned about the following:

- Using the `if` statement

- How to use Boolean logic

- `switch` statements

- Using `for`, `do`, `while`, and `for each` loops

CHAPTER 7

Methods

A *method* is a series of statements combined into one block inside a class and given a name. In the Cold War days, these were called sub-routines, and many other languages call them *functions*. However, the main difference between a method and a function is that a method has to be associated with a class, whereas a function does not.

Call Me

Methods exist to be called. You can think of a method as a message that is sent or a command given. To *call* a method (also known as *invoking* a method), you typically write the name of the object, a dot, then the method name. For example:

```
1   Dragon dragon = new Dragon();
2   dragon.fly(); // dragon is the object, and fly is the method
```

The fly method would be defined within the Dragon class.

```
1   public void fly() {
2           // flying code
3   }
```

© Adam L. Davis 2020
A. L. Davis, *Modern Programming Made Easy*,
https://doi.org/10.1007/978-1-4842-5569-8_7

Q Void   In Java, `void` means that although the method might do many things, no result is returned.

Methods can also have parameters. A *parameter* is a value (or reference value) that is part of a method call. Together, the method's name, return type, and parameters are called the *method signature*. For example, the following method has two parameters:

```
1   public void fly(int x, int y) {
2           // fly to that x, y coordinate.
3   }
```

Non-Java

Other languages define methods (or functions) differently. For example, in Groovy, you can use the def keyword to define a method (in addition to Java's normal syntax), as follows:

```
1   def fly() { println("flying") }
```

Scala also uses the def keyword to define a method, but you also need an equal (=) sign.

```
1   def fly() = { println("flying") }
```

JavaScript uses the function keyword to define a function:

```
1   function fly() { alert("flying") }
```

Break It Down

Methods also exist to organize your code. One rule of thumb is to never have a method that is longer than one screen. It makes no difference to the computer, but it makes all the difference to humans (including you).

It's also very important to name your method well. For example, a method that fires an arrow should be called "fireArrow," and not "fire," "arrow," or "arrowBigNow."

This may seem like a simple concept, but you might be surprised by how many people fail to grasp it. It also might be overlooked when you are in a hurry. If you don't name a thing well, it will make your life (and that of other programmers working with you) harder in the future.

Return to Sender

Often, you will want a method to return a result. In Java, you use the return keyword to do this. For example:

```
1    public Dragon makeDragonNamed(String name) {
2        return new Dragon(name);
3    }
```

Once the return statement is reached, the method is complete. Whatever code called the method will resume execution. If there is a return type (like the preceding Dragon), the method can return a value of that type and it can be used by the calling code (the preceding method returns a new Dragon object).

In some languages, such as Groovy and Scala, the return keyword is optional. Whatever value is put on the last line of the method will be returned. For example, in Groovy the following code is acceptable:

```
1    def makeDragonNamed(name) {
2            new Dragon(name)
3    }
```

Static

In Java, a *static method* is a method that is not linked to an object instance. It cannot refer to non-static fields of the class it is defined in. However, it must be part of a class.

For example, the random() method in the java.util.Math class we learned about earlier is a static method.

To declare a static method, you simply add the word static, as in the following code:

```
1    public static String getWinnerBetween(Dragon d, Vampire v) {
2            return "The Dragon wins";
3    }
```

For example, if the preceding method is defined in a class named Fight, it could be called from another class as Fight. getWinnerBetween(dragon, vampire) where dragon is an instance of a Dragon and vampire is an instance of a Vampire.

Because Java is an object-oriented programming (OOP) language (as well as Scala and Groovy), static methods should be used sparingly, because they are not linked to any object instance. However, they can be useful in many circumstances. For instance, they can be useful for "factory" methods (methods which create objects). The method makeDragonNamed() defined previously is a good example of a factory method. Static methods can also be useful for code that is used from many different classes; java.util.Arrays.asList() is an example—it takes any number of parameters and returns a new List containing those values.

Varargs

Varargs, or "variable arguments," allow you to declare a method's last parameter with an ellipsis (...), and it will be interpreted to accept any number of parameters of a given type (including zero parameters) and convert them into an array in your method. For example, see the following code:

```
1   void printSpaced(Object... objects) {
2           for (Object o : objects) System.out.print(o + " ");
3   }
```

Putting it all together, you can have the following code (with output in comments):

```
1   printSpaced("A", "B", "C"); // A B C
2   printSpaced(1, 2, 3); // 1 2 3
```

Main Method

Now that you know about static methods, you can finally run a Java program (sorry it took so long). Here's how you create an executable *main method* in Java (the class name can be different, but the main method must have this signature in order for Java to execute it):

```
1   import static java.lang.System.out;
2   /** Main class. */
3   public class Main {
4       public static void main(String ... args) {
5           out.println("Hello World!");
6       }
7   }
```

Then, to compile it, open your command prompt or terminal and type the following:

```
1    javac Main.java
2    java Main
```

In the groovyConsole, just press Ctrl+R.
Or in NetBeans, do the following:

- Right-click the Main class.

- Choose Run File.

Exercises

✐ Try out methods. After you've created the Main class, try adding some methods to it. Try calling methods from other methods and see what happens.

✐ Lists, Sets, and Maps   In Java, all of these data structures are under the java.util package. So, start by importing this whole package:

```
1    import    java.util.*;
```

Then go back to Chapter 5 and try out some of the code there.

Summary

This chapter explained the concept of methods and how they should be used.
We also put together everything you've learned up to this point and made a small Java application.

CHAPTER 8

Inheritance

Inheritance is a good way to share functionality between objects. When a class has a parent class, we say it *inherits* the fields and methods of its parent.

In Java, you use the extends keyword to define the parent of a class. For example:

```
1   public class Griffon extends FlyingCreature {
2   }
```

Another way to share functionality is called *composition*. This means that an object holds a reference to another object and uses it to do things. For example, see the following Griffon and Wing classes:

```
1   class Griffon {
2       Wing leftWing = new Wing()
3       Wing rightWing = new Wing()
4       def fly() {
5           leftWing.flap()
6           rightWing.flap()
7       }
8   }
9   class Wing {
10      def flap() { println 'flap'}
11  }
12  new Griffon().fly()
```

© Adam L. Davis 2020
A. L. Davis, *Modern Programming Made Easy*,
https://doi.org/10.1007/978-1-4842-5569-8_8

Running the preceding code in the groovyConsole would print out "flap flap". This way you can have a Bird class that also uses the Wing class for example.

Objectify

What is an object anyway? An *object* is an instance of a class (in Java, Groovy, and Scala). It can have state (fields, also known as instance variables) stored in memory.

In Java, classes have constructors, which can have multiple parameters for initializing the object. For example, see the following:

```
1    class  FlyingCreature  {
2            String name;
3            // constructor
4            public  FlyingCreature(String name) {
5                this.name = name;
6            }
7    }
```

The constructor of FlyingCreature has one parameter, name, which is stored in the name field. A constructor must be called using the new keyword, to create an object, for example:

```
1    String name = "Bob";
2    FlyingCreature fc = new  FlyingCreature(name);
```

Once an object is created, it can be passed around (this is called a *pass by reference*). Although String is a special class, it is a class, so you can pass around an instance of it, as shown in the preceding code.

JavaScript

In JavaScript, a constructor is a function used to define a *prototype* (a prototype in JavaScript is somewhat like a class definition in Java). Inside the constructor, the prototype is referred to using the this keyword. For example, you could define a Creature in JavaScript, as follows:

```
1  function Creature(n) {
2      this.name = n;
3  }
4  var bob = new Creature('Bob');
```

This constructor adds a name variable to the Creature prototype. The object defined earlier (bob) has the name value of 'Bob'.

Note   All functions and objects in JavaScript have a prototype.

Parenting 101

A *parent class* defines shared functionality (methods) and state (fields) that are common to multiple classes. You can specify the visibility of fields and methods using access modifiers like public and protected (we will cover these more in depth later).

For example, let's create a FlyingCreature class that defines a fly() method and has a name.

```
1  class FlyingCreature {
2          String name;
3          public FlyingCreature(String name) {
4                  this.name = name;
5          }
6          public void fly() {
```

```
7                      System.out.println(name + " is flying");
8              }
9      }
10     class Griffon extends FlyingCreature {
11             public  Griffon(String n) { super(n); }
12     }
13     class Dragon extends FlyingCreature {
14             public  Dragon(String n) { super(n); }
15     }
16     public  class  Parenting  {
17             public static void main(String ... args) {
18                     Dragon d = new  Dragon("Smaug");
19                     Griffon g = new   Griffon("Gilda");
20                     d.fly(); // Smaug is flying
21                     g.fly(); // Gilda is flying
22             }
23     }
```

There are two classes in the preceding code, Griffon and Dragon, that extend FlyingCreature. FlyingCreature is sometimes referred to as the *base class*. Griffon and Dragon are referred to as *subclasses*.

Within each constructor of Griffon and Dragon, the keyword super refers to the parent class's (FlyingCreature) constructor.

Keep in mind that you can use the parent class's type to refer to any subclass. For example, you can make any flying creature fly, as follows:

```
1    FlyingCreature creature = new Dragon("Smaug");
2    creature.fly(); // Smaug is flying
3    FlyingCreature gilda = new Griffon("Gilda");
4    gilda.fly(); //Gilda is flying
```

This concept is called *extension, inheritance, or polymorphism.* You *extend* the parent class (FlyingCreature, in this case).

JavaScript

In JavaScript, we can use prototypes to extend functionality.

For example, let's say we have a prototype called Undead.

```
1    function Undead() {
2        this.dead = false;

3    }
```

Now let's create two other constructors, Zombie and Vampire. JavaScript also has a built-in object named Object which has a create method that creates a new object based on the given prototype. For example:

```
1    function Zombie() {
2        Undead.call(this); // calls the Undead constructor
3        this.diseased = true;
4        this.talk = function() { alert("BRAINS!") }
5    }
6    Zombie.prototype = Object.create(Undead.prototype);
7
8    function Vampire() {
9        Undead.call(this); // calls the Undead constructor
10       this.pale = true;
11       this.talk = function() { alert("BLOOD!") }
12   }
13   Vampire.prototype = Object.create(Undead.prototype);
```

Note how we set Zombie's and Vampire's prototype to an instance of the Undead prototype. This allows zombies and vampires to inherit the properties of Undead while having different talk functions, as follows:

```
1   var zombie = new Zombie();
2   var vamp = new Vampire();
3   zombie.talk();    //BRAINS
4   zombie.diseased;  // true
5   vamp.talk();      //BLOOD
6   vamp.pale; //true
7   vamp.dead; //false
```

Packages

In Java (and related languages, Groovy, and Scala), a *package* is a namespace for classes. *Namespace* is just shorthand for a bin of names (names can be reused if they are in different bins). Every modern programming language has some type of namespace feature. This is necessary, owing to the nature of having lots of classes in typical projects.

As you learned in Chapter 3, the first line of a Java file defines the package of the class, for example:

```
1   package com.github.modernprog;
```

The Java file also needs to reside in the directory corresponding to the package, so in this case com/github/modernprog. Also, there is a common understanding that a package name typically corresponds to a URL (github.com/modernprog, in this case). However, this is not necessary.

Public Parts

You might be wondering why the word *public* shows up everywhere in the examples so far. The reason has to do with encapsulation. *Encapsulation* is a big word that just means "a class should expose as little as possible to get the job done" (some things are meant to be private). This helps reduce complexity of code and therefore makes it easier to understand and think about.

There are three different keywords in Java for varying levels of "exposure."

- `private`: Only this class can see it.

- `protected`: Only this class and its descendants can see it.

- `public`: Everyone can see it.

🔑 There's also "default" protection (absence of a keyword), which limits use to any class in the same package (package protected).

This is why classes tend to be declared `public`, because, otherwise, their usage would be very limited. However, a class can be private when declaring a class within another class, as follows:

```
1   public class Griffon extends FlyingCreature {
2           private class GriffonWing {}
3   }
```

JavaScript

JavaScript does not have the concept of packages, but, instead, you must rely on `scope`. Variables are only visible inside the function they were created in, except for *global* variables. There are frameworks in JavaScript for providing something like packages, but they are outside the scope of this book. One is RequireJS[1] which allows you to define modules and dependencies between modules.

Interfaces

An *interface* declares method signatures that will be implemented by classes that implement the interface. This allows Java code to work with several different classes without necessarily knowing what specific class is "underneath" the interface. An interface is something like a contract that says what an implementing class must implement.

For example, you could have an interface with one method, as follows:

```
1   public interface  Beast  {
2           int getNumberOfLegs();
3   }
```

Then you could have several different classes that *implement* that interface. Interface methods are public by default. For example:

```
1   public class Griffon extends FlyingCreature
    implements  Beast {
2           public int getNumberOfLegs() { return 2; }
3   }
4   public class Unicorn implements Beast {
5           public int getNumberOfLegs() { return 4; }
6   }
```

In Java 8, the ability to add static methods and the "default method" feature was added which allows you to implement a method within an interface. For example, you can use the default keyword and provide an

---

[1]https://requirejs.org

implementation (which can still be overridden—implemented a different way—by implementing classes):

```
1   public interface  Beast  {
2           default int getNumberOfLegs() { return 2; }
3   }
```

Note   JavaScript does not have an equivalent concept to interface; however, interfaces are not useful since JavaScript is not strongly typed. You can call any method you want.

Abstract Class

An *abstract* class is a class that can have abstract methods but cannot have instances. It is something like an interface with functionality. However, a class can only extend one superclass, while it can implement multiple interfaces.

For example, to write the preceding Beast interface as an abstract class, you can do the following:

```
1   public abstract class Beast {
2           public abstract int getNumberOfLegs();
3   }
```

Then you could add non-abstract methods and/or fields. For example:

```
1   public abstract class Beast {
2           protected String name;
3           public String getName() { return name; }
4           public abstract int getNumberOfLegs();
```

Enums

In Java, the enum keyword creates a type-safe, ordered list of constant values. For example:

```
1    public enum BloodType {
2            A, B, AB, O, VAMPIRE, UNICORN;
3    }
```

An enum variable can only point to one of the values in the enum. For example:

```
1    BloodType type = BloodType.A;
```

The enum is automatically given a bunch of methods, such as

- values(): Gives you an array of all possible values in the enum (static)

- valueOf(String): Converts the given string into the enum value with the given name (static)

- name(): An instance method on the enum that gives its name

Also, enums have special treatment in switch statements. For example, in Java, you can use an abbreviated syntax (assuming type is a BloodType).

```
1    switch (type) {
2            case VAMPIRE: return vampire();
3            case UNICORN: return unicorn();
4            default: return human();
5    }
```

Annotations

Java annotations allow you to add meta-information to Java code that can be used by the compiler, various APIs, or even your own code at runtime. They can be put before definitions of methods, classes, fields, parameters, and some other places.

The most common annotation you will see is the `@Override` annotation, which declares to the compiler that you are overriding a method from either a superclass or interface. For example:

```
1   @Override
2   public String toString() {
3           return "my own string";
4   }
```

This is useful because it will cause a compile-time error if you mistype the method name or a parameter's type for example. It's not required to override a method, but it's good practice to use it.

Other useful annotations are those in `javax.annotation`, such as `@Nonnull` and `@Nonnegative`, which can be added to parameters to declare your intentions and be used by an IDE to help catch bugs in code.

There are many other annotations used by frameworks like Hibernate, Spring Boot, and others that can be very useful. Annotations such as `@Autowired` and `@Inject` are used by direct-injection frameworks such as Spring and Google Guice[2] to reduce "wiring" code.

---

[2]`https://github.com/google/guice`

Autoboxing

Although Java is an object-oriented language, this sometimes conflicts with its primitive types (int, long, float, double, etc.). For this reason, Java added autoboxing and unboxing to the language.

Autoboxing

The Java compiler will automatically wrap a primitive type in the corresponding object when it's necessary, like int to Integer, boolean to Boolean, double to Double, and float to Float. For example, when passing in parameters to a function or assigning a variable, as in the following: Integer number = 1.

Unboxing

Unboxing is the reverse of autoboxing. The Java compiler will unwrap an object to the corresponding primitive type when possible. For example, the following code is acceptable: double d = new Double(1.1) + new Double(2.2).

Summary

After reading this chapter, you should understand OOP, polymorphism, and the definitions of the following:

- Extension and composition

- Public vs. private vs. protected vs. package protected

- Class, abstract class, interface, and enum

- Annotations

- Autoboxing and unboxing

CHAPTER 9

Design Patterns

In object-oriented programming (OOP), design patterns are useful organizations of state and behavior that make your code more readable, testable, and extensible. Now that you understand classes, inheritance, objects, and the basics of programming, let's go over some common *design patterns*—common ways of arranging application code.

Observer

The *observer* pattern allows you to broadcast information from one class to many others, without them having to know about each other directly (low coupling).

It is often used with events. For example, the `KeyListener`, `MouseListener`, and many other "Listener" interfaces in Java Swing, which is a built-in part of the JDK for building desktop applications, implement the observer pattern and use events.

Another example of this pattern is the `Observable` class and `Observer` interfaces supplied in Java. Here is a simple example that simply repeats the same event forever:

```
1    import java.util.Observable;
2
3    public class EventSource extends Observable implements
     Runnable {
4        @Override
```

© Adam L. Davis 2020
A. L. Davis, *Modern Programming Made Easy*,
https://doi.org/10.1007/978-1-4842-5569-8_9

```
5       public void run() {
6           while  (true) {
7               notifyObservers("event");
8           }
9       }
10  }
```

Although the event is a String in this example, it could be of any type.

The following class implements the Observer interface and prints out any events of type String:

```
1   import java.util.Observable;
2   import java.util.Observer;
3
4   public class StringObserver implements Observer {
5       public void update(Observable obj, Object event) {
6           if (event instanceof String) {
7               System.out.println("\nReceived Response: " +
                    event );
8           }
9       }
10  }
```

To run this example, write the following code within your main method:

```
1   final EventSource eventSource = new EventSource();
2   // create an observer
3   final StringObserver stringObserver = new StringObserver();
4   // subscribe the observer to the event source
5   eventSource.addObserver(stringObserver);
6   // starts the event thread
7   Thread thread = new  Thread(eventSource);
8   thread.start();
```

Although you are only adding one observer on line 5, you could add any number of observers without changing the code of EventSource. This is what is meant by low coupling.

MVC

Model–view–controller (MVC) is possibly the most popular software design pattern (Figure 9-1). As the name suggests, it consists of three major parts:

- *Model*: The data or information being shown and manipulated

- *View*: What actually defines how the model is shown to the user

- *Controller*: Defines how actions can manipulate the model

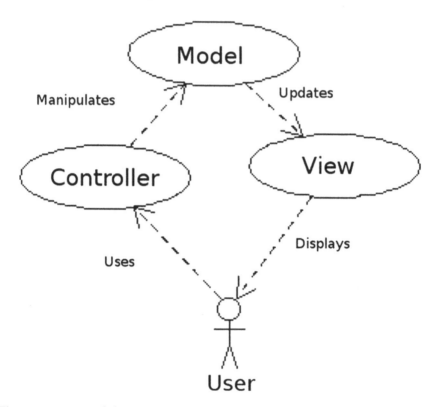

Figure 9-1. *Model–view–controller*

This design allows the controller, model, and view to know very little about each other. This reduces *coupling*—the degree to which different components of the software rely on other components. When you have low coupling, your software is easier to understand and easier to extend.

We will look at a great example of MVC in the chapter about web applications and Grails (Chapter 17).

DSL

A *domain-specific language* (DSL) is a custom programming language made for a specific domain. For example, you can think of HTML as a DSL for displaying web pages.

Some languages allow you such freedom that you can create a DSL inside the language. For example, Groovy and Scala allow you to override the math symbols (+, -, etc.). The other freedoms of these languages (optional parentheses and semicolons) allow for DSL-like interfaces. We call these DSL-like interfaces *fluent interfaces*.

You can also create fluent interfaces in Java and other languages. The following sections discuss building a DSL with Groovy.

Closures

Within Groovy, you can take a block of code (a closure) as a parameter and then call it, using a local variable as a delegate—which makes all methods of that object directly referable within the closure. For example, imagine that you have the following code for sending SMS texts:

```
1    class SMS {
2            def from(String fromNumber) {
3                    // set the from
4            }
5            def to(String toNumber) {
6                    // set the to
7            }
8            def body(String body) {
9                    // set the body of text
10           }
```

```
11              def send() {
12                      // send the text.
13              }
14    }
```

In Java, you'd have to use this the following way (notice the repetition):

```
1    SMS m = new SMS();
2    m.from("555-432-1234");
3    m.to("555-678-4321");
4    m.body("Hey there!");
5    m.send();
```

In Groovy, you can add the following static method to the SMS class for DSL-like usage (it takes a closure, sets the delegate to an instance of the SMS class, calls the block, and then calls send on the SMS instance):

```
1    def static send(Closure block) {
2            SMS m = new SMS()
3            block.delegate = m
4            block()
5            m.send()
6    }
```

This sets the SMS object as a delegate for the block, so that methods are forwarded to it. With this you can now do the following:

```
1    SMS.send {
2            from '555-432-1234'
3            to '555-678-4321'
4            body 'Hey there!'
5    }
```

Overriding Operators

In Scala or Groovy, you could create a DSL for calculating speeds with specific units, such as meters per second.

```
1   val time =  20 seconds
2   val dist =  155 meters
3   val speed =  dist / time
4   println(speed.value) //  7.75
```

By overriding operators, you can constrain users of your DSL to reduce errors. For example, accidentally typing time/dist here would cause a compilation error in this DSL.

Here's how you would define this DSL in Scala:

```
1   class Second(val value: Float) {}
2   class MeterPerSecond(val  value:  Float) {}
3   class Meter(val value: Float) {
4     def /(sec: Second) = {
5       new MeterPerSecond(value / sec.value)
6     }
7   }
8   class EnhancedFloat(value: Float) {
9     def seconds = {
10      new   Second(value)
11    }
12    def  meters = {
13      new  Meter(value)
14    }
15  }
16  implicit def enhanceFloat(f: Float) = new  EnhancedFloat(f)
```

⚷ Scala has the `implicit` keyword, which allows the compiler to do implicit conversions for you.

Notice how the divide / operator is defined just like any other method using the `def` keyword.

ⓘ In Groovy, you overload operators by defining methods with special names[1] such as `plus`, `minus`, `multiply`, `div`, etc.

Actors

The *actor design pattern* is a useful pattern for developing concurrent software. In this pattern, each actor executes in its own thread and manipulates its own data. The data cannot be manipulated by anyone else. Messages are passed between actors to cause them to change data (Figure 9-2).

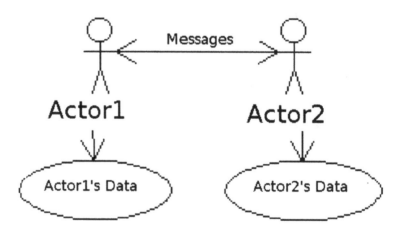

Figure 9-2. *Actors*

---

[1]`http://groovy-lang.org/operators.html#Operator-Overloading`

Note   When data can only be changed by one thread at a time, we call it *thread-safe*. If multiple threads modify the same data at the same time, this is very bad (it can cause exceptions).

There are many implementations of this pattern that you can use, including the following:

- Akka[2]

- Jetlang[3]

- FunctionalJava[4]

- GPars[5]

Chain of Responsibility

The Chain of Responsibility pattern allows you to split code up that will handle different cases without each part knowing about all the other parts.

For example, this could be a useful pattern when designing a web application that takes many different actions depending on the URL the user visits. In this case you could have a `WebHandler` interface with a method that may or may not handle that URL and returns a `String`:

```
1   public interface WebHandler {
2       String handle(String url);
3       void setNext(WebHandler next);
4   }
```

---

[2]https://akka.io
[3]https://github.com/jetlang
[4]http://functionaljava.org/
[5]http://gpars.org/

Then you can implement that interface, and call on the next handler in the chain if you do not handle that URL:

```
1   public class ZombieHandler implements WebHandler {
2       WebHandler next;
3       public String handle(String url) {
4           if (url.endsWith("/zombie")) return "Zombie!";
5           else return next.handle(url);
6       }
7       public void setNext(WebHandler next) {this.next = next;}
8   }
```

This class would only return a value if the URL ended with /zombie. Otherwise, it delegates to the next handler in the chain.

Facade

The Facade pattern allows you to hide the complexity of a larger system under a simpler design. For example, you could have one class with some methods that call the methods of many other classes.

Let's take the previous example and create a facade that handles an incoming web URL without needing to reference any specific WebHandler implementations. Create a class named WebFacade:

```
1   public class WebFacade {
2     public String handle(String url) {
3         WebHandler firstHandler = new ZombieHandler();
4         WebHandler secondHandler = new DragonHandler();
5         WebHandler finalHandler = new DefaultHandler();
6         firstHandler.setNext(secondHandler);
7         secondHandler.setNext(finalHandler);
8         return firstHandler.handle(url);
9     }
10 }
```

The WebFacade creates all of our handler classes, wires them together (calling setNext), and finally returns a value by calling the handle method of the first WebHandler.

The user of WebFacade wouldn't need to know anything about how the URL was handled. This is the usefulness of the Facade pattern.

Summary

In this chapter, you learned about some common design patterns and ways of designing applications. This is not a comprehensive list of design patterns. For more information about object-oriented design patterns, check out oodesign.com.[6] In this chapter, you learned

- What a DSL is and how to write one

- Observer, MVC, Chain of Responsibility, and Facade patterns

- Actor pattern for handling concurrency

---

[6]www.oodesign.com/

CHAPTER 10

Functional Programming

Functional programming (FP) is a programming style that focuses on functions and minimizes changes of state (using immutable data structures). It is closer to expressing solutions mathematically, rather than through step-by-step instructions.

In FP, functions should be "side-effect free" (nothing outside the function is changed) and *referentially transparent* (a function returns the same value every time when given the same arguments). For example, this would allow values to be cached (saved in memory).

FP is an alternative to the more common *imperative programming*, which is closer to telling the computer the steps to follow.

Although functional programming could be achieved in Java pre-Java-8,[1] Java 8 enabled language-level FP support with lambda expressions and *functional interfaces*.

Java 8, JavaScript, Groovy, and Scala all support functional-style programming, although they are not FP languages.

---

[1] http://functionaljava.org/

© Adam L. Davis 2020
A. L. Davis, *Modern Programming Made Easy*,
https://doi.org/10.1007/978-1-4842-5569-8_10

> **Note**   Prominent functional programming languages such as
> Common Lisp, Scheme, Clojure, Racket, Erlang, OCaml, Haskell, and
> F# have been used in industrial and commercial applications by a
> wide variety of organizations. Clojure[2] is a Lisp-like language that
> runs on the JVM.

Functions and Closures

Functions as a first-class feature is the basis of functional programming.
First-class feature means that a function can be used anywhere a value can
be used.

For example, in JavaScript, you can assign a function to a variable and
call it like the following:

```
1   var func = function(x) { return x + 1; }
2   var three = func(2); //3
```

Although Groovy doesn't have first-class functions, it has something
very similar: closures. A closure is simply a block of code wrapped in curly
brackets with parameters defined left of the -> (arrow). For example:

```
1   def closr = {x -> x + 1}
2   println( closr(2) ); //3
```

If a closure has one argument, it can be referenced as it in Groovy. For
example, the following has the same meaning as the preceding closr:

```
1   def closr = {it + 1}
```

---

[2]https://clojure.org/

Java 8 introduced the lambda expression, which is something like a closure that implements a functional interface (an interface with a single abstract method). The main syntax of a lambda expression is as follows:

```
parameters -> body
```

The Java compiler uses the context of the expression to determine which functional interface is being used (and the types of the parameters). For example:

```
1   Function<Integer,Integer> func = x -> x + 1;
2   int three = func.apply(2); //3
```

Here, the functional interface is Function<T,R>, which has the apply method—T being the parameter type and R being the return type. The return value and parameter type are both Integers, thus Integer,Integer are the generic type parameters.

⚡ In Java 8, a *functional interface* is defined as an interface with exactly one abstract method. This even applies to interfaces that were created with previous versions of Java.

In Scala, everything is an expression and functions are a first-class feature. Here's a function example in Scala:

```
1   var  f =  (x:  Int) =>  x + 1;
2   println(f(2)); //3
```

Although both Java and Scala are statically typed, Scala actually uses the right-hand side to infer the type of function being declared, whereas Java does the opposite in most cases. Java 11 introduced the local variable type **var** which allows syntax very close to Scala's **var**.

> ✑ In Java, Groovy, and Scala, the `return` keyword can be omitted, if there is one expression in the function/closure. However, in Groovy and Scala, the `return` keyword can also be omitted, if the returned value is the last expression.

Map, Filter, etc.

Once you have mastered functions, you quickly realize that you need a way to perform operations on collections (or sequences or streams) of data. Because these are common operations, *sequence operations,* such as `map`, `filter`, reduce, etc., were invented.

We'll use JavaScript for the examples in this section, because it is easier to read, and the function names are fairly standard across programming languages. Create the following `Person` prototype and `Array`:

```
1 function Person(name, age) { this.name = name; this.age = age; }
2 var persons = [new Person("Bob", 18),
3    new Person("Billy", 21), new Person("sam", 12)]
```

The map function translates or changes input elements into something else (Figure 10-1). The following code collects the names of each person:

```
1   var names = persons.map(function(person) { return person.
    name })
```

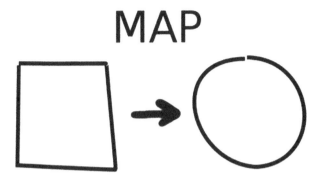

Figure 10-1. *Map*

filter gives you a subset of elements (what returns true from some *predicate* function—a function that returns a boolean given one argument [Figure 10-2]). For example, the following code collects only those persons with an age greater than or equal to 18:

```
1   var adults = persons.filter(function(person) { return
    person.age >= 18 })
```

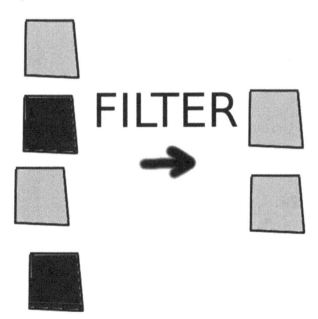

Figure 10-2. *Filter*

reduce performs a reduction on the elements (Figure 10-3). For example, the following code collects the total age of all persons:

```
1   var totalAge = persons.reduce(function(total, p) { return
    total+p.age },0)
```

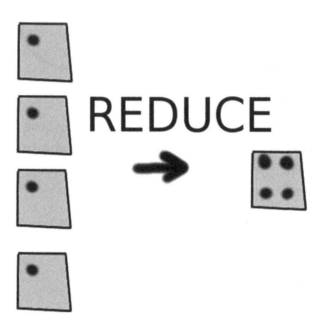

***Figure 10-3.** Reduce*

limit gives you only the first N elements (Figure 10-4). In JavaScript you can achieve this using the Array.slice(start, end) function. For example, the following code gets the first two persons:

```
1   var firstTwo = persons.slice(0, 2)
```

Figure 10-4. *Limit*

concat combines two different collections of elements (Figure 10-5). This can be done in JavaScript like the following example:

```
1 var morePersons = [new Person("Mary", 55), new Person("Sue", 22)]
2 var all = persons.concat(morePersons);
```

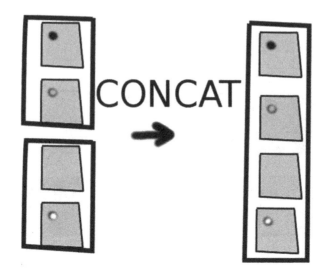

Figure 10-5. *Concat*

Immutability

Immutability and FP go together like peanut butter and jelly. Although it's not necessary, they blend nicely.

In purely functional languages, the idea is that each function has no effect outside itself—no side effects. This means that every time you call a function, it returns the same value given the same inputs.

To accommodate this behavior, there are *immutable* data structures. An immutable data structure cannot be directly changed but returns a new data structure with every operation.

For example, as you learned earlier, Scala's default Map is immutable.

```
1   val map = Map("Smaug" -> "deadly")
2   val map2 = map + ("Norbert" -> "cute")
3   println(map2) // Map(Smaug -> deadly, Norbert -> cute)
```

So, in the preceding, map would remain unchanged.

Each language has a keyword for defining immutable variables (values):

- Scala uses the val keyword to denote immutable values, as opposed to var, which is used for mutable variables.

- Java has the final keyword for declaring variables immutable (this only stops the value from being modified, if it's a reference to another object, that object's variables could still be modified).

- In addition to the final keyword, Groovy includes the @Immutable annotation[3] for declaring a whole class immutable.

- JavaScript uses the const keyword.[4]

For example (in Groovy):

```
1   public class Centaur {
2       final String name
3       public Centaur(name) {this.name=name}
4   }
5   Centaur c = new Centaur("Bane");
6   println(c.name) // Bane
7
8   c.name = "Firenze" //error
```

---

[3]http://bit.ly/32vyU8n
[4]https://mzl.la/33uOJyY

This works for simple references and primitives, such as numbers and strings, but for things such as lists and maps, it's more complicated. For these cases, open source immutable libraries have been developed for the languages in which it's not included, such as the following:

- Guava[5] for Java and Groovy

- Immutable-JS[6] for JavaScript

Java

In Java 8, the Stream<T> interface was introduced. A stream is like an improved iterator that supports chaining methods to perform complex operations.

To use a stream, you must first create one in one of the following ways:

- Collection's stream() *method or* parallelStream() *method*: These create a stream backed by the collection. Using the parallelStream() method causes the stream operations to be run in parallel.

- Arrays.stream() *method*: Used for converting arrays to streams.

- Stream.generate(Supplier<T> s): Returns an infinite sequential stream in which each element is generated by the given supplier.

---

[5]https://github.com/google/guava
[6]https://github.com/facebook/immutable-js

- `Stream.iterate(T seed, UnaryOperator<T> f)`:
  Returns an infinite sequential ordered stream
  produced by iterative application of a function to an
  initial element seed, producing a stream consisting of
  seed, f(seed), f(f(seed)), etc.

Once you have a stream, you can then use `filter`, `map`, and `reduce`
operations to concisely perform calculations on the data. For example, the
following code finds the longest name from a list of dragons:

```
1    String longestName = dragons.stream()
2         .filter(d -> d.name != null)
3         .map(d -> d.name)
4         .reduce((n1, n2) -> n1.length() > n2.length() ? n1 : n2)
5         .get();
```

Groovy

In Groovy, `findAll` and other methods are available on every object but
are especially useful for lists and sets. The following method names are
used in Groovy:

- `findAll`: Much like `filter`, it finds all elements that
  match a closure.

- `collect`: Much like `map`, this is an iterator that builds a
  collection.

- `inject`: Much like `reduce`, it loops through the values
  and returns a single value.

- `each`: Iterates through the values using the given closure.

- `eachWithIndex`: Iterates through with two parameters:
  a value and an index (the index of the value, starting at
  zero and going up).

- `find`: Finds the first element that matches a closure.

- `findIndexOf`: Finds the first element that matches a closure and returns its index.

- `any`: `True` if any element returns `true` for the closure.

- `every`: `True` if all elements return `true` for the closure.

For example, the following assumes `dragons` is a list of `Dragon` objects which have a `name` property:

```
1   String longestName = dragons
2         .findAll { it.name != null }
3         .collect { it.name }
4         .inject("") { n1, n2 -> n1.length() > n2.length() ? n1 : n2 }
```

🔍 Remember that `it` in Groovy can be used to reference the single argument of a closure.

Scala

Scala has many such methods on its built-in collections, including the following:

- `map`: Converts values from one value to another

- `flatMap`: Converts values to collections of values and then concatenates the results together (similar to the `flatten()` method in Groovy)

- `filter`: Limits the returned values, based on some Boolean expression

- `find`: Returns the first value matching the given predicate

- forAll: True only if all elements match the given predicate

- exists: True if at least one element matches the given predicate

- foldLeft: Reduces the values to one value using the given closure, starting at the last element and going left

- foldRight: Same as foldLeft, but starting from the first value and going up (similar to reduce in Java)

For example, you can use map to perform an operation on a list of values, as follows:

```
1  val list = List(1, 2, 3)
2  list.map(_ * 2) // List(2, 4, 6)
```

 Much like it in Groovy, in Scala, you can use the underscore to reference a single argument.

Assuming dragons is a List of dragon objects, you can do the following in Scala to determine the longest name:

```
1  var longestName = dragons.filter(_ != null).map(_.name).
   foldRight("")(
2      (n1:String,n2:String) => if (n1.length() > n2.length())
       n1 else n2)
```

Summary

In this chapter, you should have learned about

- Functions as a first-class feature

- Map, filter, reduce

- Immutability and how it relates to FP

- Various features supporting FPs in Java, Groovy, Scala, and JavaScript

CHAPTER 11

Refactoring

Refactoring[1] means changing code in a way that has no effect on functionality. It is only meant to make the code easier to understand or to prepare for some future addition of functionality. For example, sometimes you refactor code to make it easier to test. Many IDEs provide menus and key shortcuts for performing common refactorings.

There are two categories of refactoring we will cover, object-oriented and functional, corresponding to the two different programming styles.

Object-Oriented Refactoring

The following actions are common refactorings in OOP:

- Changing a method or class name (renaming)
- Moving a method from one class to another (delegation)
- Moving a field from one class to another
- Adding or removing parameters from a method
- Creating a new class using a set of methods and fields from a class
- Changing a local variable to a class field

---

[1]Yes refactoring is a word!

© Adam L. Davis 2020
A. L. Davis, *Modern Programming Made Easy*,
https://doi.org/10.1007/978-1-4842-5569-8_11

- Replacing a bunch of literals (strings or numbers) with a constant (static final)

- Replacing some constants or literals with an enum

- Moving a class from an anonymous class to a top-level class

- Renaming a field

Functional Refactoring

The following actions are common refactorings in FP:

- Renaming a function

- Wrapping a function in another function and calling it

- Inline a function wherever it is called

- Extract common code into a function (the opposite of the previous)

- Renaming a function parameter

- Adding or removing a parameter

You might notice some similarities between both lists. The principles of refactoring are universal.

Refactoring Examples

NetBeans, like many IDEs, supports refactoring. You can try it out by selecting some code, right-clicking, and selecting the *Refactor* menu. Here are some examples of refactoring code.

Renaming a Method

Before:

```
1   public static void main(String...args) {
2       animateDead();
3   }
4   public  static void  animateDead() {}
```

After:

```
1   public static void main(String...args) {
2       doCoolThing();
3   }
4   public  static void  doCoolThing() {}
```

Moving a Method from One Class to Another (Delegation)

Before:

```
1   public static void main(String...args) {
2       animateDead();
3   }
4   public  static void  animateDead() {}
```

After:

```
1   public class Animator() {
2       public void animateDead() {}
3   }
4   public static void main(String...args) {
5       new Animator().animateDead();
6   }
```

Replacing a Bunch of Literals (Strings or Numbers) with a Constant (Static Final)

Before:

```
1   public static void main(String...args) {
2       animateDead(123);
3       System.out.println(123);
4   }
5   public static void animateDead(int n) {}
```

After:

```
1   public static final int NUM = 123;
2   public static void main(String...args) {
3       animateDead(NUM);
4       System.out.println(NUM);
5   }
6   public static void animateDead(int n) {}
```

Renaming a Function

Before:

```
1   function castaNastySpell() { /* cast a spell here */ }
```

After:

```
1   function castSpell() { /* cast a  spell here  */ }
```

Wrapping a Function in Another Function and Calling It

Before:

```
1   castSpell('my cool spell');
```

After:

```
1   (function(spell) { castSpell(spell) })('my cool spell');
```

Inline a Function Wherever It Is Called

This might be done during refactoring when a function is too simple or is only used in one place.

Before:

```
1   function castSpell(spell) { alert('You cast ' + spell); }
2   castSpell('crucio');
3   castSpell('expelliarmus');
```

After:

```
1   alert('You cast ' + 'crucio');
2   alert('You cast ' + 'expelliarmus');
```

Extract Common Code into a Function (the Opposite of the Previous)

Before:

```
1   alert('You cast crucio');
2   alert('You cast expelliarmus');
```

After:

```
1   function castSpell(spell) { alert('You cast ' + spell); }
2   castSpell('crucio');
3   castSpell('expelliarmus');
```

CHAPTER 12

Utilities

There are many classes, functions, or objects (sometimes called utilities) that come built-in with each programming language that can be very useful. The `java.util` package contains many useful classes for everyday programming. Likewise, JavaScript and other languages come with many built-in objects for doing common tasks. I am going to cover a few of these.

Dates and Times

You should never store date values as text. It's too easy to mess up (Figure 12-1).

***Figure 12-1.** I can has string to store date valyooz?*

© Adam L. Davis 2020
A. L. Davis, *Modern Programming Made Easy*,
https://doi.org/10.1007/978-1-4842-5569-8_12

Java Date-Time

Java 8 introduced a new and improved date-time application program interface (API) in the `java.time` package that is much safer, easier to read, and more comprehensive than the previous API.

For example, creating a date looks like the following:

```
1    LocalDate date = LocalDate.of(2014, Month.MARCH, 2);
```

There's also a `LocalDateTime` class to represent date and time, `LocalTime` to represent only time, and `ZonedDateTime` to represent a time with a time zone.

Before Java 8, there were only two built-in classes to help with dates: `Date` and `Calendar`. These should be avoided when possible.

- `Date` actually represents both a date and time.

- `Calendar` is used to manipulate dates.

In Java 7 and lower, you would have to do the following to add five days to a date:

```
1    Calendar cal = Calendar.getInstance();
2    cal.setTime(date);
3    cal.add(5, Calendar.DAY);
```

Whereas in later versions of Java, you could do the following:

```
1    LocalDate.now().plusDays(5)
```

Groovy Date

Groovy has a bunch of built-in features that make dates easier to work with. For example, numbers can be used to add/subtract days, as follows:

```
1    def date = new Date() + 5; //adds 5 days
```

Groovy also has TimeCategory[1] for manipulating dates and times. This lets you add and subtract any arbitrary length of time. For example:

```
1   import groovy.time.TimeCategory
2   now = new Date()
3   println now
4   use(TimeCategory) {
5       nextWeekPlusTenHours = now + 1.week + 10.hours - 30.seconds
6   }
7   println nextWeekPlusTenHours
```

A Category is a class that can be used to add functionality to other existing classes. In this case, TimeCategory adds a bunch of methods to the Integer class.

CATEGORIES

This is one of the many *meta-programming* techniques available in Groovy. To make a category, you create a bunch of static methods that operate on one parameter of a particular type (e.g., Integer). When the category is used, that type appears to have those methods. The object on which the method is called is used as the parameter. Take a look at the documentation for TimeCategory for an example of this in action.

---

[1]http://docs.groovy-lang.org/latest/html/api/groovy/time/TimeCategory.html

JavaScript Date

JavaScript also has a built-in Date[2] object.

You can create an instance of a Date object in several ways (these all create the same date):

```
1   Date.parse('June 13, 2014')
2   new Date('2014-06-13')
3   new Date(2014, 5, 13)
```

Note that if you adhere to the international standard (yyyy-MM-dd), a UTC time zone will be assumed; otherwise, it will assume you want a local time.

As usual with JavaScript, the browsers all have slightly different rules, so you have to be careful with this.

⚠ **Don't ever use getYear!**   In both Java and JavaScript, the Date object's getYear method doesn't do what you think and should be avoided. For historical reasons, getYear does not actually return the year (e.g., 2014). You should use getFullYear() in JavaScript and LocalDate or LocalDateTime in Java.

Java DateFormat

Although DateFormat is in java.text, it goes hand in hand with java.util.Date.

---

[2]http://mzl.la/1unepot

The SimpleDateFormat is useful for formatting dates in any format you want. For example:

```
1   SimpleDateFormat sdf = new  SimpleDateFormat("MM/dd/yyyy");
2   Date date = new  Date();
3   System.out.println(sdf.format(date));
```

This would format a date per the US standard: month/day/year.

Java 8 introduced the java.time.format.DateTimeFormatter to format or parse using the new date and time classes. Each java.time class, such as LocalDate, has a format method and a static parse method which both take an instance of DateTimeFormatter.

For example:

```
1   LocalDate date = LocalDate.now();
2   DateTimeFormatter formatter = DateTimeFormatter.
    ofPattern("MM/dd/yyyy");
3   String text = date.format(formatter);
4   LocalDate parsedDate = LocalDate.parse(text, formatter);
```

⚙ More Formatting   See the documentation for SimpleDateFormat[3] for more information about it. See the DateTimeFormatter[4] documentation for more about it.

---

[3]https://docs.oracle.com/javase/8/docs/api/java/text/SimpleDateFormat.html

[4]https://docs.oracle.com/javase/8/docs/api/java/time/format/DateTimeFormatter.html

Currency

In Java, `java.util.Currency` is useful if your code has to deal with currencies in several countries. It provides the following methods:

- `getInstance(Locale)`: Static method to get an instance of Currency based on Locale

- `getInstance(String)`: Static method to get an instance of Currency based on a currency code

- `getSymbol()`: Currency symbol for the current locale

- `getSymbol(Locale)`: Currency symbol for the given locale

- `static getAvailableCurrencies()`: Returns the set of available currencies

For example:

```
1   String pound = Currency.getInstance(Locale.UK).getSymbol();
    // GBP
2   String dollar = Currency.getInstance("USD").getSymbol(); // $
```

TimeZone

In Java 8 and above, time zones are represented by the `java.time.ZoneId` class. There are two types of ZoneIds, fixed offsets and geographical regions. This is to compensate for practices such as daylight saving time, which can be very complex.

You can get an instance of a ZoneId in many ways, including the following two:

```
1   ZoneId mountainTime = ZoneId.of("America/Denver");
2   ZoneId myZone = ZoneId.systemDefault();
```

To print out all available IDs, use getAvailableZoneIds(), as follows:

```
1   System.out.println(ZoneId.getAvailableZoneIds());
```

✒ Write a program that does this and run it. For example, in the groovyConsole, write the following and execute:

```
import java.time.*
println(ZoneId.getAvailableZoneIds())
```

Scanner

Scanner can be used to parse files or user input. It breaks the input into tokens, using a given pattern, which is whitespace by default ("whitespace" refers to spaces, tabs, or anything that is not visible in text).

For example, use the following to read two numbers from the user:

```
1   System.out.println("Please type two numbers");
2   Scanner sc = new Scanner(System.in);
3   int num1 = sc.nextInt();
4   int num2 = sc.nextInt();
```

✒ Write a program that does this and try it out. Since this requires input, it can't be done with the groovyConsole. Use either NetBeans to build a Java application or a Groovy script you run with groovy on the command line.

97

CHAPTER 13

Building

The *build process* is typically one of compiling the source files of a project, running tests, and producing a finished product or products.

In some companies there are whole teams whose sole job is maintaining and updating the build process. In any project of any size, it helps to have a good automated build tool.

There are many other build tools, but we're just going to cover three:

- Ant[1]

- Maven[2]

- Gradle[3]

Ant

Ant is the first really popular project builder for Java that existed. It is XML-based and requires you to create tasks in XML that can be executed by Ant. An Ant build file is typically named `build.xml` and has a `<project>` root element.

---

[1]http://ant.apache.org
[2]http://maven.apache.org
[3]https://gradle.org

© Adam L. Davis 2020
A. L. Davis, *Modern Programming Made Easy*,
https://doi.org/10.1007/978-1-4842-5569-8_13

A *task* is a division of work. Tasks depend on other tasks. For example, the `jar` task usually depends on the `compile` task. Although Maven threw away the task concept, it was used again in Gradle.

Critics of Ant complain that it uses XML (a declarative and highly verbose format) and requires a lot of work to do simple things. However, it was a very popular tool for many years and is still used in many places.

Maven

Maven is an XML-based declarative project manager. Maven is used for building Java projects but is capable of much more. Maven is also a set of standards that allows Java/JVM developers to easily define and integrate dependencies into large projects. Maven somewhat replaces Ant but can also integrate with it and other build tools.

Maven was mostly a reaction to the huge number of open source libraries Java projects tend to rely on. It has a built-in standard for dependency management (managing the inter-dependencies of open source libraries).

Although Maven is an Apache open source project, it could be said that the core of Maven is *Maven Central*, a repository of open source libraries run by *Sonatype*, the company behind Maven. There are many other repositories that follow the Maven standard, such as JFrog's jCenter,[4] so you are not restricted to Maven Central.

Note   Ivy[5] is a similar build tool, but is more closely related to Ant.

---

[4]https://bintray.com/bintray/jcenter
[5]http://ant.apache.org/ivy/

Many build tools, such as Ivy and Gradle, build on top of Maven's concept.

Using Maven

The main file that defines a Maven project is the *POM* (Project Object Model). The POM file is written in XML and contains all of the dependencies, plug-ins, properties, and configuration data that is specific to the current project. The POM file is generally composed of the following:

- Basic properties (`artifactId`, `groupId`, `name`, `version`, `packaging`)

- Dependencies

- Plug-ins

There is a Maven plug-in for every major Java-based IDE out there (Eclipse, NetBeans, and IntelliJ IDEA), and they are very helpful. You can use the Maven plug-in to create your project, add dependencies, and edit your POM files.

Starting a New Project

There is a simple way to create a new configuration file (`pom.xml`) and project folders using the `archetype:generate` command.

```
mvn archetype:generate
```

That will list all the different kinds of projects you can create. Pick a number representing the type of project you want (there are thousands of options right now), then answer some questions, such as the name of your project. After that process, run the following command to build the project:

```
1   mvn package
```

If you want to use any additional third-party libraries, you will have to edit the POM to include each dependency. Fortunately, most IDEs make it easy to add dependencies to the POM.

ⓘ *Maven: The Complete Reference*[6] is available online if you want to learn more.

Life Cycle

Maven uses a declarative style (unlike Ant, which uses a more imperative approach). This means that instead of listing the steps to take, you describe what should happen during certain phases of the build. The phases in Maven are built in and are listed as follows (and execute in this order):

1. `validate`: Validates that the project is correct and all necessary information is available

2. `compile`: Compiles the source code of the project

3. `test`: Tests the compiled source code, using a suitable unit-testing framework

4. `package`: Takes the compiled code and packages it in its distributable format, such as a JAR

5. `integration-test`: Processes and deploys the package, if necessary, into an environment in which integration tests can be run

6. `verify`: Runs any checks to verify that the package is valid and meets quality criteria

---

[6]`www.sonatype.com/ebooks`

7. `install`: Installs the package into the local repository, for use as a dependency in other projects locally

8. `deploy`: Copies, in an integration or release environment, the final package to the remote repository, for sharing with other developers and projects

---

ℹ️ There are more phases,[7] but you don't need to know all of them until you are doing more complex builds.

Executing Code

Sometimes, however, you just need more control over your build. In Maven, you can execute Groovy code, Ant build files, and Scala code, and you can even write your own plug-ins in Groovy.

For example, you can put Groovy code in your POM file in the following way:

```
1   <plugin>
2    <groupId>org.codehaus.groovy.maven</groupId>
3    <artifactId>gmaven-plugin</artifactId>
4    <executions>
5     <execution>
6      <id>groovy-magic</id>
7      <phase>prepare-package</phase>
8      <goals>
9        <goal>execute</goal>
```

---

[7]https://maven.apache.org/guides/introduction/introduction-to-the-lifecycle.html#Lifecycle_Reference

```
10        </goals>
11          <configuration>
12            <source>
13              def depFile =
14              new File(project.build.outputDirectory, 'deps.txt')
15              project.dependencies.each {
16                depFile.write(
17                    "${it.groupId}:${it.artifactId}:${it.
                    version}")
18              }
19              ant.copy(todir: project.build.outputDirectory ) {
20                fileset(dir: project.build.sourceDirectory)
21              }
22            </source>
23          </configuration>
24        </execution>
25      </executions>
26    </plugin>
```

The preceding code would write out every dependency of the project into the file deps.txt. Then it would copy all of the source files into the project.build.outputDirectory (usually target/classes).

ℹ️ See Chapters 2, 3, and 4 in *The Maven Cookbook*.[8]

---

[8]http://books.sonatype.com/mcookbook/reference/index.html

Gradle

Gradle is an automated build tool with a Groovy native DSL (domain-specific language) for defining project builds. It also has a Kotlin native DSL and is the official build tool for Android projects.

The Gradle web site has this to say about Gradle as of writing:

From mobile apps to microservices, from small startups to big enterprises, Gradle helps teams build, automate and deliver better software, faster.

—gradle.org[9]

Getting Started with Gradle

To get started easily, you can use Gradle's built-in init plugin. After installing Gradle, run the following command:

```
gradle init
```

When prompted you can choose a Java application with Junit 4 tests and a Groovy build script (type 2, enter, 3, enter, 1, enter, 1, enter). This will create a build.gradle file, a settings.gradle file, gradlew, and gradlew.bat (which allow you to run Gradle from any system without even installing it) and some basic code and a test.

Projects and Tasks

Each Gradle build is composed of one or more projects and each project is composed of one or more tasks.

---

[9]https://gradle.org/

The *core* of the Gradle build is the build.gradle file, which is called the *build script*. Tasks can be defined by writing task, then a task name, followed by a closure. For example:

```
1   task upper doLast {
2           String someString = 'test'
3           println "Original: $someString"
4           println "Uppercase: " + someString.toUpperCase()
5   }
```

Much as in Ant, a task can depend on other tasks, which means they must be run before the task. You can specify dependsOn with any number of task names as a List within your task definition. For example:

```
1   task buildApp(dependsOn: [clean, jar]) {
2       // define task here
3   }
```

Tasks can contain any Groovy code (or Kotlin if using the Kotlin DSL), but you can take advantage of some of the many existing Gradle plugins to quickly produce a dependable and fast build.

Plugins

Gradle core has very little built-in. It has powerful plugins which allow it to be very flexible. A plugin can do one or more of the following:

- Add tasks to the project (e.g., compile, test).

- Pre-configure added tasks with useful defaults.

- Add dependency configurations to the project.

- Add new properties and methods to existing type, via extensions.

We're going to concentrate on building Java-based projects, so we'll be using the java plugin; however, Gradle is not limited to Java projects.

For example, at the beginning of your build.gradle file, you should see something like the following code:

```
1   plugins {
2       id 'java'
3       id 'application'
4   }
```

This enables the java plugin and the application plugin.

Gradle uses standard project organization conventions. For example, it expects to find your production Java source code under src/main/java and your test Java source code under src/test/java. This is the same style expected by Maven.

Dependencies

Every Java project tends to rely on many open source projects to be built. Gradle builds on the concepts that came before it, so you can easily define your dependencies using a simple DSL, such as in the following example:

```
1    plugins { id 'java' }
2
3    sourceCompatibility = 1.11
4
5    repositories {
6        mavenLocal()
7        mavenCentral()
8    }
9
10   dependencies {
11       implementation 'com.google.guava:guava:23.0'
```

107

```
12      implementation 'io.reactivex.rxjava2:rxjava:2.2.10'
13      testImplementation group: 'junit', name: 'junit',
        version: '4.12+'
14      testImplementation "org.mockito:mockito-core:1.9.5"
15   }
```

This build script uses sourceCompatibility to define the Java source code version of Java 11 (which is used during compilation). Next, it tells Maven to use the local repository first (mavenLocal), then Maven Central.

In the dependencies block, this build script defines two dependencies for the implementation scope and two for testImplementation scope. Jars in the testImplementation scope are only used in tests and won't be included in any final products.

The line for JUnit shows the more verbose style for defining dependencies. The "+" here means that version or greater.

Do First and Last

You can use doFirst and doLast to specify code that should run before and after your tasks. For example, let's take our task from earlier and add some additional code:

```
1  task buildApp(dependsOn: [clean, jar]) {
2      doFirst { println "starting to build" }
3      doLast { println "done building" }
4  }
```

This would print out "starting to build" before the task is run and "done building" after it completes. Type `gradle buildApp` in your command prompt to run this task. You should see output much like the following:

```
> Task :buildApp
starting to build
done building

BUILD SUCCESSFUL in 983ms
4 actionable tasks: 4 executed
```

Your jar file will now be located in the `build/libs/` directory of your project.

ℹ️   Gradle has a huge online user guide available online at gradle.org.[10]

---

[10]https://docs.gradle.org/current/userguide/userguide.html

CHAPTER 14

Testing

Testing is a very important part of the software creation process. Without automated tests, it's very easy for bugs to creep into software.

In fact, some go as far as to say that you should write tests *before* you write the code. This is called *TDD* (test-driven development).

There are multiple test frameworks and tools to help you test your code. This book will cover some of these tools, JUnit and Spock.

Types of Tests

The following are different types of tests you might write:

- *Unit test*: Test conducted on a single API call or some isolated code or component

- *Integration test*: Test of a larger system that integrates together two or more components

- *Acceptance test*: High-level test that matches the business requirements

- *Compatibility*: Making sure that things work together

- *Functionality*: Ensuring that stuff works

- *Black box*: Test conducted without knowing/thinking about what's going on in the code

© Adam L. Davis 2020
A. L. Davis, *Modern Programming Made Easy*,
https://doi.org/10.1007/978-1-4842-5569-8_14

- *White box*: Tests written with the inside of code in mind

- *Gray box*: Hybrid of black and white box testing

- *Regression*: Creating a test after finding a bug, to ensure that the bug does not reappear

- *Smoke*: A huge sampling of data use during a test

- *Load/stress/performance*: How the system handles load (a lot of traffic to a web site for example)

The type and number of tests you write vary, based on a number of factors. The simpler a piece of code is, the less testing it requires. For example, a getter or setter does not require a test by itself.

JUnit

JUnit[1] is a simple framework to write repeatable tests.

A typical JUnit test consists of multiple methods annotated with the @Test annotation.

At the top of every JUnit test class, you should include the following imports:

```
1   import static org.junit.jupiter.api.Assertions.*;
2   import org.junit.jupiter.api.Test;
3   import org.junit.jupiter.api.BeforeEach;
4   import org.junit.jupiter.api.AfterEach;
```

Use @BeforeEach to annotate initialization methods that are run before every test and @AfterEach to annotate breakdown methods that are run after every test. The methods should ensure that each test is independent.

---

[1]https://junit.org/junit5/

Each test method should test one thing, and the method name should reflect the purpose of the test. For example:

```
1   @Test
2   public void mapSizeIsCorrect() {
3

    Map<String,String> map = new HashMap<>();
4        map.put("Smaug", "deadly");
5        map.put("Norbert", "cute");
6        assertEquals(2, map.size());
7   }
```

The first parameter to the assertEquals method is what is expected, and the second parameter is the actual value to test. When the two values are not equal, this will throw an Exception and the test will fail. A failing test means our expectations were not met by the code. The software should be considered incorrect at this point and not go any further until the test is successful (not failing).

Hamcrest

You can create more readable tests using the Hamcrest core matchers. In JUnit you must import Hamcrest[2] matchers separately. You can import them as follows:

```
1   import static org.hamcrest.CoreMatchers.equalTo;
2   import static org.hamcrest.CoreMatchers.is;
3   import static org.hamcrest.MatcherAssert.assertThat;
```

Here's an example of using a Hamcrest matcher:

```
1   @Test
2   public void sizeIs10() {
3            assertThat(map.size(), is(2));
4   }
```

This test would assert that map's size is 2. There are many other matchers and you can even build your own.

Assumptions

Often, there are variables outside of a test that are beyond your control but which your test assumes to be true. When an assumption fails, it shouldn't necessarily mean that your test fails. For this purpose, JUnit added Assumptions, which you may import like so:

```
1   import static org.junit.jupiter.api.Assumptions.*;
```

You can verify assumptions before your assertions in your tests. For example, if the following is put at the beginning of a test, the rest of that test would only run on a system with "/" as the file separator (i.e., not Windows):

```
1   assumeTrue(File.separatorChar, is('/'));
```

When an assumption fails, the test is either marked as passing or ignored, depending on the version of JUnit.[3]

---

[3]http://junit.sourceforge.net/doc/ReleaseNotes4.4.html

Spock

Spock is a testing framework for Java, Groovy, or any other JVM language. It takes full advantage of Groovy and has object mocking built-in. The Spock web site[4] has this to say about Spock:

> What makes it stand out from the crowd is its beautiful and highly expressive specification language. Thanks to its JUnit runner, Spock is compatible with most IDEs, build tools, and continuous integration servers. Spock is inspired from JUnit, RSpec, jMock, Mockito, Groovy, Scala, Vulcans, and other fascinating life forms.

Spock Basics

Test classes in Spock are called *Specifications*. The basic structure of a Specification in Spock is a class that extends `spock.lang.Specification` and has multiple test methods (which may have descriptive String names). The class's name should end with `Spec`, for example, a Specification about a `Vampire` class could be named `VampireSpec`.

Spock processes the test code and allows you to use a Groovy-based syntax to specify tests. Spock tests should go under the `src/test/groovy` directory.

Each test is composed of labeled blocks of code with labels like `when`, `then`, and `where`. The best way to learn Spock is with examples.

---

[4]`https://code.google.com/p/spock/`

To get started, first add Spock as a dependency to your project. For example, within a Gradle build file, put the following:

```
1   dependencies {
2     testImplementation "org.spockframework:spock-core:1.3-
        groovy-2.5"
3   }
```

A Simple Test

Let's start by recreating a simple test:

```
1   def "toString yields the String representation"() {
2           def array = ['a', 'b', 'c'] as String[]
3           when:
4           def arrayWrapper = new ArrayWrapper<String>(array)
5           then:
6           arrayWrapper.toString() == '[a, b, c]'
7   }
```

As shown, assertions are simply Groovy conditional expressions. Every line after then: will be tested for Groovy truthiness. If the == expression returns false, the test will fail and Spock will give a detailed printout to explain why it failed.

In the absence of any when clause, you can use the expect clause instead of then; for example:

```
1   def "empty list size is zero"() {
2           expect: [].size() == 0
3   }
```

Mocking

Mocking is when you use a tool to extend an interface or class that can mimic the behavior of that class or interface within a test to assist testing your code. In JUnit tests, you need to use a library, like *Mockito*,[5] to mock other classes that are not part of the test.

Mocking interfaces or classes is extremely easy in Spock.[6] Simply use the Mock method, as shown in the following example (where Subscriber is an interface):

```
1   class APublisher extends Specification {
2     def publisher = new Publisher()
3     def subscriber = Mock(Subscriber)
```

Now subscriber is a mocked object. You can implement methods simply using the overloaded >> operator as shown next. The following example throws an Exception whenever receive is called:

```
1   def "can cope with misbehaving subscribers"() {
2       subscriber.receive(_) >> { throw new Exception() }
3
4       when:
5       publisher.send("event")
6       publisher.send("event")
7
8       then:
9       2 * subscriber.receive("event")
10  }
```

---

[5]https://site.mockito.org/

[6]You can also Mock classes, but it requires including the bytebuddy JAR as a dependency: testRuntime "net.bytebuddy:byte-buddy:1.10.1".

Expected behavior can be described by using a number or range multiplied by (*) the method call, as shown here (it expects the receive method should be called two times).

The underscore (_) is treated like a wildcard (much like in Scala).

Lists or Tables of Data

Spock allows you to use lists or tables of data to more simply test multiple test cases within one test.

For example:

```
1   def "subscribers receive published events at least once"(){
2       when: publisher.send(event)
3       then: (1.._) * subscriber.receive(event)
4       where: event << ["started", "paused", "stopped"]
5   }
```

The overloaded << operator is used to provide a list for the event variable. Although it is a list here, anything that is Iterable could be used. This has the effect of running the test for each value in the list.

⚲ Ranges   The range 1.._ here means "one or more" times. You can also use `_..3, for example, to mean "three or fewer" times.

Tabular formatted data can be used as well. For example, the following test has a table with two columns, name and length:

```
1   def "length of NASA mission names"() {
2       expect:
3       name.size() == length
4
5       where:
```

```
6          name       | length
7          "Mercury"  | 7
8          "Gemini"   | 6
9          "Apollo"   | 6
10    }
```

In this case, the two columns (name and length) are used to substitute the corresponding variables in the expect block. Any number of columns can be used.

You can also add the @Unroll annotation so that each table row results in a separate test output. You can then use # to refer to a column. For example, change the previous test's signature to the following:

```
1    @Unroll
2    def "length of NASA mission name, #name"() {
```

Expecting Exceptions

Use the thrown method in the then block to expect a thrown Exception.

```
1    def "peek on empty stack throws"() {
2        when: stack.peek()
3        then: thrown(EmptyStackException)
4    }
```

You can also capture the thrown Exception by simply assigning it to thrown(). For example:

```
1    def "peek on empty stack throws"() {
2        when: stack.peek()
3        then:
4        Exception e = thrown()
5        e.toString().contains("EmptyStackException")
6    }
```

After writing some tests, run the tests with either Gradle or Maven. For Gradle run `./gradlew test` (results go under `build/reports/tests/test/`). For Maven run `mvn test` (results are under `build/surefire-reports/`).

Other Test Frameworks

There are many other test frameworks that unfortunately we do not have time to cover. Some are used to enable automated browser testing of web applications, like Geb[7] and Selenium.[8]

Others enable BDD (behavior-driven development) like Cucumber.[9] Cucumber enables tests to be written in close to plain English. For example, a scenario for testing some code from earlier in the book:

```
Scenario: Longest Dragon name
  Given a list of Dragons
  When the longest Dragon name is found
  Then the name is "Norbert"
```

Summary

In this chapter, you've learned how testing is a very important part of software development and the types of tests you should write. You've learned about how to use JUnit and Spock for running tests and learned that other test frameworks exist for running integration tests or BDD.

---

[7]`https://gebish.org/`
[8]`www.seleniumhq.org/`
[9]`https://cucumber.io/`

CHAPTER 15

Input/Output

Many times when developing an application, you need to read or write from files or a network connection. These things are generally referred to as input and output or I/O for short.

In this chapter, we will cover some of the utilities available for I/O within Java and the JVM.

Files

In Java, the `java.io.File` class is used to represent files and directories. For example:

```
1   File file = new  File("path/file.txt");
2   File dir = new File("path/"); //directory
```

Java 7 added several new classes and interfaces for manipulating files and file systems under the `java.nio` package. This new application program interface (API) allows developers to access many low-level OS operations that were not available from the Java API before, such as the `WatchService` and the ability to create links (in Linux/Unix operating systems).

Paths are used to more consistently represent file or directory paths.

```
1   Path path = Paths.get("/path/file");
```

© Adam L. Davis 2020
A. L. Davis, *Modern Programming Made Easy*,
https://doi.org/10.1007/978-1-4842-5569-8_15

This is shorthand for the following:

```
1   Path path = FileSystems.getDefault().getPath("/path/file");
```

The following list defines some of the most important classes and interfaces of the API:

> Files: This class consists exclusively of static methods that operate on files, directories, or other types of files.

> Paths: This class consists exclusively of static methods that return a path by converting a path string or URI.

> WatchService: An interface for watching various file system events, such as create, delete, and modify.

Reading Files

To read a text file in Java, you can use BufferedReader. For example:

```
1   public void readWithTry() {
2     Charset utf = StandardCharsets.UTF_8;
3     try (BufferedReader reader = Files.newBufferedReader
      (path, utf)) {
4       for (String line = br.readLine(); line!=null; line =
        br.readLine())
5           System.out.println(line);
6     } catch (IOException e) {
7         e.printStackTrace();
8     }
9   }
```

The *automatic resource management* feature of Java makes dealing with resources, such as files, much easier. Before Java 7, programmers needed to explicitly close all open streams, causing some very verbose code. By using the preceding try statement, BufferedReader will be closed automatically.

However, in Groovy, this can be reduced to one line (leaving out exception handling), as follows:

```
1   println path.toFile().text
```

A getText() method is added to the File class in Groovy that simply reads the whole file. A getBytes() method is also available for reading bytes from a file.

Writing Files

Writing files is similar to reading them. For writing to text files, you should use PrintWriter. It includes the following methods (among others):

- print(Object): Prints the given object directly calling toString() on it

- println(Object): Prints the given object and then a newline

- println(): Prints the newline character sequence

- printf(String format, Object...args): Prints a formatted string using the given input

For example, you can use PrintWriter to easily write to a file as follows:

```
1   public void printWithTry() {
2           try (FileOutputStream fos = new
            FileOutputStream("books.txt");
```

```
3                    PrintWriter pw = new PrintWriter(fos)) {
4                        pw.println("Modern Java");
5                } catch (IOException e) {
6                        // log the exception
7                }
8    }
```

There are other ways to output to files, such as DataOutputStream, for example:

```
1    public void writeWithTry() {
2            try (FileOutputStream fos = new
             FileOutputStream("books.txt");
3                    DataOutputStream dos = new
                    DataOutputStream(fos)) {
4                        dos.writeUTF("Modern Java");
5                } catch (IOException e) {
6                        // log the exception
7                }
8    }
```

DataOutputStream allows an application to write primitive Java data types to an output stream. You can then use DataInputStream to read the data back in. If you're just dealing with text, you can use PrintWriter and BufferedReader instead.

In Groovy, you can more easily write to files, as follows:

```
1    new File("books.txt").text = "Modern Java"
2    new File("binary.txt").bytes = "Modern Java".bytes
```

Groovy adds a setText method and a setBytes to the File class, which allows this syntax to work.

Downloading Files

Although you might not ever do this in practice, it's fairly simple to download a web page/file in code.

The following Java code opens an HTTP connection on the given URL (https://www.google.com, in this case), reads the data into a byte array, and prints out the resulting text.

```
1   URL url = new URL("https://www.google.com");
2   InputStream input = (InputStream) url.getContent();
3   ByteArrayOutputStream out = new ByteArrayOutputStream();
4   int n = 0;
5   byte[] arr = new  byte[1024];
6
7   while  (-1 != (n = input.read(arr)))
8       out.write(arr, 0, n);
9
10  System.out.println(new String(out.toByteArray()));
```

However, in Groovy, this also can be reduced to one line (leaving out exceptions).

```
1   println "https://www.google.com".toURL().text
```

A toURL() method is added to the String class, and a getText() method is added to the URL class in Groovy.

Summary

After reading this chapter, you should understand how to

- Explore the file system in Java

- Read from a file

- Write to a file

- Download the Internet

CHAPTER 16

Version Control

As soon as people start their programming careers, they are hit with the ton of bricks that is the version control system (VCS).

Version control software is used to keep track of, manage, and secure changes to files. This is a very important part of modern software development projects.

This book is going to cover two popular ones (but there are many more):

- SVN (Subversion)
- Git (git)

Every VCS has the following basic actions:

- Add
- Commit
- Revert
- Remove
- Branch
- Merge

IDEs have plug-ins for dealing with version control systems and usually have built-in support for popular systems such as SVN and Git.

© Adam L. Davis 2020
A. L. Davis, *Modern Programming Made Easy*,
https://doi.org/10.1007/978-1-4842-5569-8_16

Subversion

SVN[1] was made as an improvement to an ancient and very popular VCS called CVS. It was a huge leap forward. Among other benefits, it allows any directory in the hierarchy to be checked out of the system and used. SVN requires a server to store the history, tags, and branches of the code. Programmers then use the SVN client to commit code changes.

To begin using SVN on the command line, you will check out a project and then commit files, for example:

```
1   svn checkout http://example.com/svn/trunk
2   svn add file
3   svn commit
```

Git

Git[2] is a distributed version control system. This means that every copy of the source code contains the entire history of the code. However, unlike most other systems, it stores the history in a very compact and efficient and secure way—each commit is associated with a *hash* (a compact, but unique value generated from larger values by a one-way algorithm). It was initially created by the creator of Linux (Linus Torvalds) and is very popular.

To begin using Git on a new project, simply run the following command:

```
1   git init
```

---

[1]https://subversion.apache.org/
[2]https://git-scm.com/

Create a file called README and then commit it, as follows:

```
1    git add README
2    git commit -m "this is my comment"
```

✏️ Install Git. Go to github.com[3] and clone a repository, for example, git clone https://github.com/adamldavis/learning-groovy.git. Now create your own GitHub account, create a new repository, clone it, and follow the preceding instructions to add a new file to it. Lastly, use git push to push the changes to GitHub.

When you have a remote host set up in your local git repository (like when you cloned a repository from GitHub), you are able to push changes to it and pull changes from it. For example, the git push command pushes your commits to the remote host, and the git pull command gets changes from the host (that other developers might have put there).

Other helpful commands:

- git log: Shows all commits, most recent first

- git status: Shows the current status of your git repository

- git show: Given a commit hash, shows all changes of that commit

- git checkout: Given a branch name, loads that branch

- git merge: Joins two or more development histories together

---

[3]https://github.com/

- `git branch`: Can be used to list, create, or delete branches

- `git tag`: Can be used to list, create, or delete tags

- `git help`: Gives you helpful documentation. Gives help specific command when used like `git help <command>`

Mercurial

Mercurial[4] predates Git but is very similar to it. It's used for a lot of projects on Google Code and Bitbucket.[5]

✏ Install Mercurial. Go to Bitbucket and clone a repository using Mercurial, for example, `hg clone https://bitbucket.org/adamldavis/dollar`.

---

[4]www.mercurial-scm.org
[5]https://bitbucket.org/

CHAPTER 17

The Interweb

(Courtesy xkcd: Interblag)

© Adam L. Davis 2020
A. L. Davis, *Modern Programming Made Easy*,
https://doi.org/10.1007/978-1-4842-5569-8_17

Just about all software projects are now Internet-based, either web applications (those that produce HTML that is shown via a browser like Firefox) or web services (those that connect via JavaScript in the browser or through mobile apps, like those on Android and iOS devices).

This chapter is devoted to learning about the concepts and some code related to web applications and web services.

Web 101

The Web is a complex beast. Here's what you need to know:

- *Server*: The computer serving web pages and other content

- *Client*: The computer that receives web pages and is used by a person

- *Request*: The data sent to the Server from the Client

- *Response*: The data sent back to the Client after a Request

- *HTML*: The language used to define web pages

- *CSS*: "Cascading style sheets"; defines the styles of the web page

- *JavaScript*: A programming language that is used within web pages and executed on the client, although it can be used on the server side as well

My First Web App

You should make something very basic for your first web application. This way, you will have a better understanding of what's going on "behind the scenes" of many web frameworks. A *web framework* is a set of related tools and libraries useful for building web applications.

Create a file called App.java and copy the following code into it:

```
 1    import java.io.IOException;
 2    import java.io.OutputStream;
 3    import java.net.InetSocketAddress;
 4    import com.sun.net.httpserver.*;
 5
 6    public class App {
 7
 8        static class MyHandler implements HttpHandler {
 9            public void handle(HttpExchange t) throws
              IOException {
10                String response = "<html> Hello Inter-webs!
                  </html>";
11                t.sendResponseHeaders(200, response.length());
12                OutputStream os = t.getResponseBody();
13                os.write(response.getBytes());
14                os.close();
15            }
16        }
17
18        public static void main(String[] args) throws Exception {
19            HttpServer server = HttpServer.create(new
              InetSocketAddress(8000), 0);
20            server.createContext("/", new MyHandler());
21            server.setExecutor(null); // creates a default executor
```

```
22              server.start();
23              System.out.println("Server running at http://
                localhost:8000");
24      }
25
26  }
```

All this does is create an HttpServer that listens for connections on port 8000 and responds with a message.

After running this code (javac App.java && java App), open your web browser and point it to http://localhost:8000/ (it should show "Hello Inter-webs!"). Press Ctrl+C to stop the application.

Q localhost refers to the computer you're on, and :8000 refers to port 8000.

Congratulations! You just made a web application! It's not on the Internet yet, and it's extremely simple, but it's a good start.

PORT?

URL (Uniform Resource Locator): The unique name used to locate resources on any network or machine. Sometimes it starts with "http"; sometimes it includes a port.

HTTP Hypertext Transfer Protocol: The typical protocol used to communicate over the wire.

HTTPS (Secure HTTP): Similar to HTTP but encodes all data using an asymmetrical key so no device can read the data except for the intended recipient.

Port: A number that must be specified when communicating between computers (the default port for HTTP is 80).

The Holy Grails

Grails is a web framework for Groovy that follows the example of Ruby on Rails (hence *Grails*). It is an opinionated web framework with a command-line tool that gets things done really fast. Grails uses convention over configuration to reduce configuration overhead. This can greatly reduce the effort required to get started on a new project or add additional functionality.

Grails lives firmly in the Java ecosystem and is built on technologies such as Spring Boot and Hibernate. Grails also includes an object-relational mapping (ORM) framework, which maps objects to database tables, called *GORM,* and has a large collection of plug-ins.

Quick Overview

This overview is based on Grails 4.0.0, but the basics should remain the same for all versions of Grails, 3.0 and above. After installing Grails,[1] you can create an app by running the following on the command line:

```
1    $ mkdir g4
2    $ cd g4
3    $ grails create-app --inplace
```

Then, you can run commands such as `create-domain-class` and `generate-all` to create your application as you go. Run `grails help` to see the full list of commands available. We will cover these commands more fully later on in the chapter.

---

[1]`https://grails.org/download.html`

Grails applications have a very specific project structure. The following is a simple breakdown of *most* of that structure:

- `grails-app`: The Grails-specific folder.

    - `conf`: Configuration files, such as application.yml and logback.groovy.

    - `controllers`: Controllers with methods for index/create/edit/delete, or anything else.

    - `domain`: Domain model; classes representing your persistent data.

    - `i18n`: Message bundles, useful for supporting multiple languages (English, Spanish, etc.).

    - `init`: Contains your `Application.groovy` and `Bootstrap.groovy` files that initialize the application when it starts.

    - `services`: Back-end services in which your back end or "business" logic goes.

    - `taglib`: You can very easily define your own tags for use in your GSP files.

    - `views`: Views of MVC; typically, these are GSP files (HTML-based with embedded Groovy code).

- `assets`

    - `stylesheets`: CSS.

    - `images`: Images used by your web application.

    - `javascripts`: Your JavaScript files.

- src: Common code that doesn't fit anywhere else.

    - main/groovy: Groovy code.

    - test/groovy: Groovy tests.

- gradle: Contains the Gradle wrapper jar.

To create new domain (model) classes, use the create-domain-class command. Run the following (in the root directory of the project):

```
1   $ grails create-domain-class example.Comment
2   $ grails create-domain-class example.User
3   $ grails create-domain-class example.Post
```

It's a good idea to include a package for your domain classes (such as example.Post). This command creates both the domain class and an associated Spock Specification. Change User and Comment to look like the following:

```
1   class User { String name }
2   class Comment { String text }
```

A domain class in Grails also defines its mapping to the database. For example, edit your domain class representing a blog post to look like the following (assuming User and Comment have already been created):

```
1   class Post {
2       String text
3       int rating
4       Date created = new Date()
5       User createdBy
6
7       static hasMany = [comments: Comment]
8
9       static constraints = {
```

```
10              text(size:10..500)
11      }
12   }
```

The static hasMany field is a map that represents one-to-many relationships in your database—this means a Post can have many Comments. Grails uses Hibernate in the background to create tables for all your domain classes and relationships. Every table gets an id field for the primary key by default which is automatically assigned.

To have Grails automatically create your controller and views (and tests) after you have defined the domain classes, run the following:

```
1   $ grails generate-all example.User
2   $ grails generate-all example.Comment
3   $ grails generate-all example.Post
```

⚠ Grails will ask if you want to overwrite existing files, if they exist. So, be careful when using this command.

When you want to test your app, you simply run the following:

```
1   $ grails run-app
```

It should output eventually the following:

Grails application running at http://localhost:8080 in environment: development.

Next, open a browser and go to that URL. You should see the following based on the default generated views which has a list of Controllers, Application Status, Artefacts, and a list of Installed Plugins:

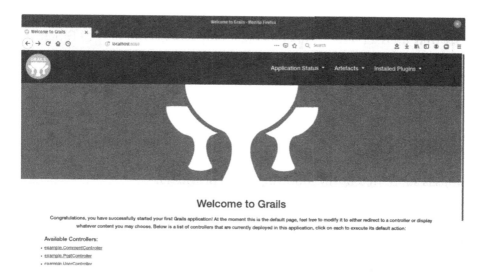

If you follow the links to the respective controllers, you can create Users, then create Posts, and then create Comments on those Posts.

Plug-ins

The Grails 4.0 system now includes over 190 plug-ins. To list all of the plug-ins, simply execute the following:

```
1    $ grails list-plugins
```

When you've picked out a plugin you want to use, execute the following to see more information about the plugin (with the plugin name):

```
1    $ grails plugin-info [NAME]
```

This will tell you how to add the plug-in to your project. Edit your build.gradle file and add the dependency there.

ℹ **Only an Overview**   This has been only a brief overview of Grails. Many books have been written about Grails and how to use it. For more information on using Grails, please visit `grails.org`.[2]

Cloud

Grails is supported by the following cloud providers:

- CloudFoundry[3]

- Amazon[4]

- Heroku[5]

However, it is not within the scope of this book to go over all of them, but we will shortly discuss *Heroku*.

Heroku was one of the first cloud platforms and has been in development since June 2007. When it began, it supported only Ruby, but it has since added support for Java, Scala, Groovy, Node.js, Clojure, and Python. Heroku supports multiple tiered accounts, including a free account.

Heroku relies on `git` for pushing changes to your server. For example, to create an app in Heroku using the CLI, do the following:

```
1   $ heroku create
2   $ git push heroku master
```

---

[2]https://grails.org/
[3]www.cloudfoundry.org/
[4]https://aws.amazon.com/ec2/
[5]www.heroku.com/

Your app will be up and running, and Heroku will identify the URL where you will find it.

 Go launch a Grails app on Heroku!

The REST

REST stands for REpresentational State Transfer.[6] It was designed in a PhD dissertation and has gained huge popularity as the new web service standard. Many developers have praised it as a much better standard than SOAP (which I will not attempt to describe).

At the most basic level in REST, each *CRUD* (create, read, update, delete) operation is mapped to an HTTP method. For example:

- *Create*: POST

- *Read*: GET

- *Update*: PUT

- *Delete*: DELETE

The transport mechanism is assumed to be HTTP, but the message contents can be of any type, usually XML or JSON.

The JSR community has designed the JAX-RS API for building RESTful Java web services, while Groovy and Scala both have some built-in support for XML and JSON and various ways of building web services. Spring Boot[7] and Spring MVC also have great support for REST.

---

[6]`www.ics.uci.edu/~fielding/pubs/dissertation/top.htm`
[7]`https://spring.io/`

Using Maven Archetypes

You can create a simple Java REST (JAX-RS) application using Maven, as follows:

```
1    mvn archetype:generate
```

Wait for things to download and then choose "tomcat-maven-archetype (type tomcat-maven and press Enter, then type "1"; Enter; Enter). You will need to enter a groupId and artifactId.

After creating your application, you can start it by typing the following command:

```
1    mvn tomcat:run
```

Using Grails JSON Views

Grails has a plugin for rendering views as JSON. First run plugin-info to see how to include it in your build:

```
1    $ grails plugin-info views-json
```

After adding it to your Grails project's build dependencies, you can use a Groovy DSL to define how to render your responses in JSON. See the documentation[8] for more information.

---

[8]http://views.grails.org/latest/

As a summary, JSON views allows you to define views under the grails-app/views directory with the .gson extension that can use a DSL for producing JSON rather than the .gsp files which produce HTML. This is useful when writing a web service that produces JSON for example.

Create a file named grails-app/views/hello.gson with the following:

```
json.message {
    hello "world"
}
```

This would produce {"message":{ "hello":"world"}} as JSON.

Summary

Congratulations! You now understand the Interweb. Yes, it *is* a series of tubes. Ted Stevens (see following) was right!

> *...They want to deliver vast amounts of information over the Internet. And again, the Internet is not something that you just dump something on. It's not a big truck. It's a series of tubes. And if you don't understand, those tubes can be filled and if they are filled, when you put your message in, it gets in line and it's going to be delayed by anyone that puts into that tube enormous amounts of material, enormous amounts of material.*

> —Theodore "Ted" Fulton Stevens, Sr., US senator from Alaska, December 24, 1968–January 3, 2009

CHAPTER 18

Swinging Graphics

Swing is the Java API for building cross-platform GUIs (graphical user interfaces).

If you ever want to write a graphical program (a computer game, for example), you will have to use Swing, or JavaFX, or something similar.

There are many other libraries for doing graphics in Java, but Swing is built in.

Hello Window

The most basic concept of graphics is getting stuff onto the screen.

The easiest way to do this in Swing is to use JWindow, for example:

```
1    import javax.swing.*; import java.awt.Graphics;
2
3    public class HelloWindow extends JWindow {
4
5        public HelloWindow() {
6            setSize(500, 500); //width, height
7            setAlwaysOnTop(true);
8            setVisible(true);
9        }
10
11        @Override
```

© Adam L. Davis 2020
A. L. Davis, *Modern Programming Made Easy*,
https://doi.org/10.1007/978-1-4842-5569-8_18

145

```
12          public void paint(Graphics g) {
13                  g.setFont(g.getFont().deriveFont(20f));
14                  g.drawString("Hello Window", 10, 20); //x,y
15          }
16
17          public static void main(String[] args) {
18                  new HelloWindow();
19          }
20
21  }
```

Running this code will create a window at the top left of your screen, with the words "Hello Window" printed on it. It should look like Figure 18-1.

Figure 18-1. *The Hello Window*

In the constructor, the following occurs:

- The width and height of the window are both set to 500 pixels.

- The window is set to always be displayed (above all other windows) with the setAlwaysOnTop method.

- Finally, setVisible(true) is called to make the window visible.

The paint method gets called every time the window is drawn on the screen. This method simply does the following:

- Sets the font size to 20

- Draws the string "Hello World" at coordinates x=10, y=20 (coordinates are always in pixels)

You might notice that the "window" doesn't have any edges, header, menu, or minimize/maximize icons that you're used to (to close it, you need to press *Ctrl+C*). To get these things, you use a JFrame. Here's a very simple example:

```
1    import javax.swing.*;
2
3    public class HelloFrame extends JFrame {
4
5            public HelloFrame() {
6                    super("Hello");
7                    setSize(500, 500); //width, height
8                    setAlwaysOnTop(true);
9                    setVisible(true);
10                   setDefaultCloseOperation(EXIT_ON_CLOSE);
11           }
12
```

```
13          public static void main(String[] args) {
14                  new HelloFrame();
15          }
16
17  }
```

Running this code creates a 500×500 "window with frame" with the name "Hello" (Figure 18-2), and closing the window would exit the application.

Figure 18-2. *A window with a JFrame*

Push My Buttons

Buttons are one of the ways that users can interact with your program. To cause something to happen when a button is pressed, you use an ActionListener, for example:

The showMessageDialog method of JOptionPane is similar to JavaScript's alert method, in that it shows a pop-up window.

```
1    button.addActionListener(e -> JOptionPane.
     showMessageDialog(this, "Hello!"));
```

This uses a Java lambda expression since ActionListener has one abstract method and thus is a functional interface as we learned earlier.

The Groovy syntax is slightly different (it only requires a { and }).

```
1    button.addActionListener({e -> JOptionPane.
     showMessageDialog(this, "Hello!")})
```

Swing has many interfaces that end with the word Listener, such as

- KeyListener

- MouseListener

- WindowListener

The *Listener* pattern is very similar to the *Observer* design pattern.

Fake Browser

Let's make a web browser!

Let's begin by adding the imports necessary:

```
1    import java.awt.*;
2    import java.awt.event.*;
3    import java.io.*;
4    import java.net.*;
5    import javax.swing.*;
```

Then let's continue by creating the fields and constructor for the class, as follows:

```
1   public class Browser extends JFrame {
2
3           JTextField urlField = new JTextField();
4           JEditorPane viewer = new JEditorPane();
5           JScrollPane pane = new JScrollPane();
6
7           public Browser() {
8                   super("Browser");
9                   setSize(800,600);
10                  setAlwaysOnTop(true);
11                  setDefaultCloseOperation(EXIT_ON_CLOSE);
12                  init();
13          }
```

JTextField will be used to input the URL. JEditorPane is used to show the HTML, and the JScrollPane allows the page to be scrollable.

Next, we define the init() method to put everything together.

```
1   private void init() {
2           viewer.setContentType("text/html");
3           pane.setViewportView(viewer);
4           JPanel panel = new JPanel();
5           panel.setLayout(new BorderLayout(2,2));
6           panel.add(pane, BorderLayout.CENTER);
7           panel.add(urlField, BorderLayout.NORTH);
8           setContentPane(panel);
9           urlField.addKeyListener(new KeyAdapter() {
10                  @Override
11                  public void keyReleased(KeyEvent e) {
12                          handleKeyPress(e);
```

```
13                          }
14              });
15    }
```

The viewer is set as the viewport view of the JScrollPane, so it can be scrolled.

JPanel is created with a BorderLayout. This allows us to arrange urlField on top of the scroll pane, much as in a real browser. KeyListener is used to call handleKeyPress whenever a key is pressed inside urlField.

Next, we fill out the handleKeyPress method.

```
1   private void handleKeyPress(KeyEvent e) {
2           if (e.getKeyCode() == KeyEvent.VK_ENTER) {
3                   try {
4                           viewer.setPage(new URL(urlField.
                            getText()));
5                   } catch (MalformedURLException ex) {
6                           ex.printStackTrace();
7                   } catch (IOException ex) {
8                           ex.printStackTrace();
9                   }
10          }
11   }
```

This method simply sets the page of JEditorPane to the URL from urlField whenever the Enter key is pressed.

Finally, we define the main method.

```
1   public static void main(String[] args) {
2   new  Browser().setVisible(true);
3   }
```

Run your app from Chapter 17. Open your fake browser, and point it to the app at http://localhost:8000/. It should look like Figure 18-3.

Figure 18-3. *Running the fake browser*

Griffon

Griffon[1] is a desktop application platform inspired by Grails. It's written in Java, so it can be used from pure Java, but using Groovy adds additional capabilities.

To get started, first install Lazybones[2] and Gradle. You can install them using the following commands:

```
$ curl -s http://get.sdkman.io | bash
$ sdk install lazybones
$ sdk install gradle
```

---

[1]http://griffon-framework.org/
[2]https://github.com/pledbrook/lazybones

Next edit the lazybones config file to add the `griffon-lazybones-templates` repository. Edit **$USER_HOME/.lazybones/config.groovy** and put the following:

```
bintrayRepositories = [
    "griffon/griffon-lazybones-templates",
    "pledbrook/lazybones-templates"
]
```

To begin a new project type, use the following:

```
$ lazybones create griffon-swing-groovy griffon-example
```

This will create a project using Groovy and Swing and named `griffon-example`. Fill in appropriate responses to each prompt (it will ask you to supply a package, version, class name, and other values). Use the `lazybones list` command to see what other types of projects are possible.

Griffon uses the MVC design pattern and Groovy DSL to make it much easier to build Swing applications.

Advanced Graphics

Although far beyond the scope of this book, there are several libraries that can be used for 2D or 3D graphics. Here are some of them:

Java 2D

- JavaFX[3]

- JFreeChart[4]

- Piccolo2D[5]

---

[3]https://openjfx.io/
[4]www.jfree.org/jfreechart/
[5]http://piccolo2d.org/

- JMagick[6]

Java 3D

- JOGL[7]

- JMonkeyEngine[8]

JavaScript 2D

- D3.js[9]

- Highcharts[10]

JavaScript 3D

- three.js[11]

Graphics Glossary

Component: Any graphical element defined in the Java graphics API.

Double buffering: A technique used in graphics in which elements are drawn in memory before being sent to the computer screen. This avoids flicker.

Frame: In Swing, the frame (JFrame) is used to represent what we typically call a "window" in the GUI.

GUI: Graphical user interface.

---

[6]https://github.com/techblue/jmagick
[7]http://download.java.net/media/jogl/www/
[8]https://jmonkeyengine.org/
[9]https://d3js.org/
[10]www.highcharts.com/
[11]https://threejs.org/

Layout: Strategy used by Swing for arranging components within a panel or other component.

Menu: There are two kinds of menus: a windows built-in menu (JMenu) and a pop-up menu (JPopupMenu).

Menu item: In Swing, the JMenuItem represents one line of a menu that can have an action associated with it.

Panel: In Swing, JPanel is used to contain other components.

Pixel: Smallest unit of the screen that is drawable. A typical screen has millions of pixels that are arranged in a grid.

Window: Rectangular section of the screen. In Swing, the Window object has no border, so it can be used for a splash image, for example.

Summary

You just learned the following:

- Creating a cross-platform GUI in Java and Groovy
- How to make a web browser worse than IE
- Some of the available graphics libraries

CHAPTER 19

Creating a Magical User Experience

First, to begin learning about designing applications with the user experience in mind, you should be aware of the following acronyms:

> *UX*: User experience. The total experience of using an application

> *UI*: User interface. The web page or graphical interface used by the user

> *KISS*: Keep it simple, stupid. An overall design concept

> *RWD*: Responsive Web Design (an approach to web design allowing web pages to render in many different devices)

Application Hierarchy

You should prioritize your UX according to the following characteristics, from highest to lowest:

1. *Functionality*: Software does what it should.

2. *Usefulness*: Is the software easy to use?

© Adam L. Davis 2020
A. L. Davis, *Modern Programming Made Easy*,
https://doi.org/10.1007/978-1-4842-5569-8_19

3. *Efficiency*: Can the user work efficiently?

4. *Magicalness*: Is the experience magical?

You can't focus on being usable if your software is not functional. You can't focus on being efficient if your software is not usable.

After you have mastered all the basics (functionality, usability, and efficiency), only then can you attempt to make your UI magical.

Consider Your Audience

It's always important to consider the audience for your software. You should get to know them as much as possible.

Those of you familiar with Harry Potter (or magic, in general) will recognize the words *wizard/witch* and *muggle*. In Potter's world, a *squib* is someone who's aware of magic but not able to practice it, and a muggle is a normal person who's unaware of magic.

We can apply this analogy to software. When designing your software, you need to keep in mind every type of person that might use it:

- *Beginning user*: Muggle

- *Proficient user*: Squib

- *Highly proficient user*: Wizard/witch

For example, if you design only for witches and wizards, the muggles will feel lost. If you design only for muggles, the witches and wizards will feel the software is incomplete and too simple.

Choice Is an Illusion

The more choices a person has, the more thinking they are required to do. As a designer, you should do the following:

- Limit choices.

- Prepare for every possible choice.

- Tailor choices for your audience.

- Validate user input, making sure it meets expectations.

You will often have to decide whether to give your user a choice or make the choice for them.

The easy way (for you) is always to let the user decide, but the better way is generally to give the user one less choice. This will make your software simpler and, therefore, easier to use.

Direction

Work instinctively—instinct is your friend. Motion is a subtle and effective way of getting the user's attention. However, too much motion is a distraction, so it should be kept to a minimum.

Another instinctual visual is the human face. Faces are noticed first. This is why you always see faces on the left-hand side of text (in languages that read from left to right). The eye is drawn first to the face and then to the accompanying text.

Skeuomorphism

Skeuomorph is something from real life that is imitated in software.

Simulating real-life features, such as edges, bevels, and buttons, can be useful for communicating *affordability* (what the user can do with something). However, you have to get it 100% right, if you're simulating a complete object (such as a book). This is why skeuomorphism is generally a bad idea. Imitating something from the real world comes across as fake, if it is not done perfectly.

You could take the opposite approach and attempt to remove all metaphor. The UI can be very flat and edgeless. However, you can take this concept too far. For example, what is clickable should still be obvious.

Context Is Important

Three stars with no context could mean anything. However, given context (3/5 stars), what is meant becomes obvious.

Context is also important for navigation. It must be obvious where the user is in your software at all times and how to navigate somewhere else. Otherwise, your users will feel lost, which is not a comfortable feeling.

A related concept is to avoid "modes." The more ways there are to interact with the software, the more complex it will seem.

KISS

Above all, keep things simple—simple for the user. For example, in general, there should always be one way to do something in the software. Also, as a general rule, your UI should follow the conventions set by existing software/web sites (e.g., always underline links).

As your software grows, you will constantly have to make choices about new UI features. In addition to other considerations, you should also contemplate how they can be made simpler.

You Are Not the User

Unless you are building software only for yourself, the overwhelming probability is that your users are very different from you. For this reason, you must not only try to think like your user but also really get to know him or her. This means ideally that you sit down and watch your users operate the software.

Likewise, in a production system you should monitor what your users are doing. Are they using that new feature? Are they doing something unexpected. Metrics can be helpful to analyze your users' behavior.

Summary

From this chapter, you should have learned the following:

- Your UI should be functional, usable, and efficient, in that order.

- Consider who your user is during all phases of design.

- Limit choices and handle all conditions.

- Instinct is your friend, but don't imitate reality.

- Keep things simple for users and listen to them.

For more about usability, I highly recommend Steve Krug's *Don't Make Me Think* (New Riders, 2014).

CHAPTER 20

Databases

Databases are an extremely important component of most software projects. In short, a database is a software system that stores data in a standardized format, and depending on the database, it might enable one or more of the following: quick storage and retrieval, the ability to perform complex queries, validation of data input, and calculations on the data.

The classic style of database going back many decades is known as a *relational database*. In addition to raw data, it stores relationships between tables in the database. A database typically consists of several highly structured data tables with defined constraints. For example, each column of a table has a type, whether or not it can be null, if it must be unique, and other constraints.

There is a highly standardized language for performing operations and calculations on a database called *SQL* (Structured Query Language). SQL has been around a long time and could easily warrant its own book, so this book will only cover the basics.

Since the advent of so-called big-data products and web applications (such as a particular "face"-themed social network), a second category of databases has emerged: *NoSQL* or *non-relational* databases. Typically these are more like key-value or document stores than relational databases. They include databases like Redis, MongoDB, Cassandra, DynamoDB, and many others.

© Adam L. Davis 2020
A. L. Davis, *Modern Programming Made Easy*,
https://doi.org/10.1007/978-1-4842-5569-8_20

> **Note**   The SQL/NoSQL categorization is an oversimplification, but it provides an easier narrative than the actual complex reality. In other words, "Here be dragons!"

SQL (Relational) Databases

Part of classic relational databases is the concept of ACID[1] (atomicity, consistency, isolation, durability). To summarize ACID, it means that the database is always in a consistent state (with enforced constraints), even if the system crashes in the middle of an update. For example, if a column in a table is marked as "not null," it will never be null. It also enables *transactions*, which are atomic units of work—either all of it happens or none of it. This may seem at first glance like a simple thing to achieve, but it is actually a very complex problem.

In relational databases the main store of data is called a table. A table has *columns* which are part of the table schema (definition) and define what kind of data specifically is stored. A table has *rows*, which is data stored in the table, and each row has values defined for each column.

---

[1]https://en.wikipedia.org/wiki/ACID.

⚲ Some good open source databases include PostgreSQL, MySQL, and H2. For this section, you can follow along by installing PostgreSQL. On Debian or Ubuntu Linux type "`sudo apt install postgresql`". For other systems, see the web site[2] for installation instructions. A good graphical tool for connecting to and manipulating databases is DBeaver.[3]

SQL

The basic language of relational databases is SQL. It includes the ability to define tables and perform complex queries on those tables.

For example, creating a table looks something like the following:

```
1   CREATE TABLE dragon(
2       dragon_id INTEGER,
3       dragon_name VARCHAR(100),
4       birth_date DATE NOT NULL,
5       PRIMARY KEY (dragon_id)
6   );
```

A table always needs to have a primary key—it acts as the identifier for each row of the table so it must be unique per row in the table. In this case, the primary key is dragon_id.

---

[2]`www.postgresql.org/download/`
[3]`https://dbeaver.io/`

Next, you can add data to the table using insert statements. For example, in PostgreSQL you can insert two rows in the following way:

```
insert into dragon values (1, 'Smaug', current_date);
insert into dragon values (2, 'Drago', current_date);
```

Database types cover the basics, such as INTEGER, but other unfamiliar types include the following:

- VARCHAR(length) is similar to the String object. It has a given maximum length.

- TIMESTAMP is used to store dates and times.

- NUMERIC(precision, scale) or DECIMAL(precision, scale) is used to store numbers such as currency values (e.g., the number 123.45 has a precision of 5 and a scale of 2).

- BLOB is typically used to store binary data.

The select statement allows you to specify which columns you want to extract from one or more tables. You can also use aggregation functions like MIN, MAX, or COUNT within a select statement to perform more complex queries. For example, to find the birthday of your oldest dragon, you might perform the following query:

```
1    SELECT MIN(birth_date) FROM dragon;
```

A where clause can be used to restrict your query to certain rows in a table. To select all dragons whose names start with S (in alphabetic order), run the following:

```
1    SELECT dragon_id, dragon_name FROM dragon
2        WHERE dragon_name LIKE 'S%'
3        ORDER BY dragon_name;
```

The order by clause is used to order the results returned from the query. The like keyword is used to match a varchar column against a matching expression where % matches any values.

Foreign Keys

A *foreign key* is simply a column in a table that references the primary key of another table.

For example, let's say you have a wizard table, and each wizard has multiple dragons they keep as pets.

```
1   CREATE TABLE wizard(
2       wizard_id INTEGER,
3       wizard_name VARCHAR(100),
4       PRIMARY KEY (wizard_id)
5   );
```

If the wizard table's primary key is wizard_id, the dragon table could have the following new definition with the owner column and foreign key constraint:

```
1   CREATE TABLE dragon(
2       dragon_id INTEGER,
3       dragon_name VARCHAR(100),
4       birth_date DATE NOT NULL,
5       PRIMARY KEY (dragon_id)
6       owner INTEGER,
7       FOREIGN KEY owner REFERENCES wizard (wizard_id)
8   );
```

Although SQL keywords are shown in uppercase, this is not required by PostgreSQL but is only for illustration purposes.

Connections

A database system typically runs as a separate process, and your code connects to it in some way.

There are many different ways to do this. In Java, the most basic standard for connecting to databases is called JDBC.

It allows you to run SQL statements on the database. You will need a specific *Driver—a library that implements the JDBC standard*—for your database.

In a real-world application, you should also use a JDBC connection pool such as HikariCP.[4] A connection pool allows connections to be reused by your application many times, which increases throughput and performance of your application since connections take time to start up.

There are also *object-relational mapping* (ORM) frameworks, such as Hibernate.[5] These frameworks have you map Java objects to data tables. They are built *on top of* JDBC. For example, Hibernate has its own query language, called HQL, which is translated into SQL by Hibernate. GORM, which we discussed earlier, uses Hibernate by default.

Alternatively, there are code-generating frameworks that allow you to use a DSL for queries. One such framework for Java is jOOQ.[6] It allows you to write type-safe queries in the native language. For example:

```
1   create.selectFrom(DRAGON)
2     .where(DRAGON.NAME.like("S%"))
3     .orderBy(DRAGON.NAME)
```

---

[4]https://github.com/brettwooldridge/HikariCP
[5]http://hibernate.org/orm/
[6]www.jooq.org/

NoSQL (Non-relational) Databases

Big web projects (such as Wikipedia) had problems using relational databases to scale up to millions of users. They had to partition their database onto multiple machines (called *sharding*), which broke foreign key references. There is a theorem about this, CAP theorem which says you can have two of consistency, availability, and partitioning in a database, but not all three. So, over time, big-data projects moved to NoSQL or non-relational databases, which make different trade-offs so they can be scaled up more easily. Many times the trade-off is *eventual consistency* rather than full consistency. In other words, one user might read an old value for a short period of time after another user input a newer value.

NoSQL databases are used by Netflix, Reddit, Twitter, GitHub, Pinterest, eBay, eHarmony, craigslist, and many others.

Note   I will cover some NoSQL databases here, but there are many others.

Redis

Redis[7] is a key-value store. Everything is stored as a string in Redis, including binary data. It's written in C and has a long list of commands.[8]

There are multiple clients for using Redis from many different languages, including Java, Node.js, Scala, Ruby, Python, and Go.

---

[7]https://redis.io/
[8]https://redis.io/commands

MongoDB

MongoDB[9] is a document database. It stores JSON-style (JavaScript) documents and has a rich query syntax. It's written in C++, but JavaScript can be used in queries and aggregation functions.

MongoDB supports indexing of any field in a document. It scales horizontally using sharding and provides high availability and increased throughput using replication. More recently it added support for ACID transactions.

MongoDB can also be used as a file system.

Cassandra

Cassandra[10] was originally developed at Facebook and was released as an open source project in July 2008. It's written in Java and is now a mature, top-level Apache project.

Cassandra is scalable, decentralized, fault tolerant, and has tunable consistency. It also uses replication for fault tolerance and performance.

Cassandra has an SQL-like alternative called *CQL* (Cassandra Query Language). Language drivers are available for Java (JDBC), Python (DBAPI2), and Node.JS (Helenus).

VoltDB

VoltDB[11] provides a counter-example to the SQL/NoSQL divide. It's distributed, in-memory, and lightning-fast, but it's also a relational database and supports SQL.

---

[9]www.mongodb.org/
[10]http://cassandra.apache.org/
[11]www.voltdb.com/

Summary

- There are two major types of databases: SQL and NoSQL or relational and non-relational.

- Relational (SQL) databases are highly structured, consistent, and durable, but difficult to scale up.

- Big-data projects tend to use non-relational databases, which are like key-value stores that can be scaled up more easily.

APPENDIX A

Java/Groovy[1]

Feature	Java	Groovy
Public class	`public class`	`class`
Loops	`for(Type it : c){...}`	`c.each {...}`
Lists	`List list = Arrays.asList(1,2,3);`	`def list = [1,2,3]`
Maps	`Map m = ...; m.put(x,y);`	`def m = [x: y]`
Function def.	`void method(Type t) {}`	`def method(t) {}`
Mutable value	`Type t`	`def t`
Immutable value	`final Type t`	`final t`
Null safety	`(x == null ? null : x.y)`	`x?.y`
Null replacement	`(x == null ? "y" : x)`	`x ?: "y"`
Sort	`Collections.sort(list)`	`list.sort()`
Wildcard import	`import java.util.*;`	`import java.util.*`
Var-args	`(String... args)`	`(String... args)`
Type parameters	`Class<T>`	`Class<T>`
Equals	`a.equals(b)`	`a == b`

---

[1]Version 2 of this cheat sheet.

© Adam L. Davis 2020
A. L. Davis, *Modern Programming Made Easy*,
https://doi.org/10.1007/978-1-4842-5569-8

No Java Analog

Feature	Groovy
Default closure arg.	`it`
Default value	`def method(t = "yes")`
Add method to object	`t.metaClass.method = {}`
Auto-delegate	`@Delegate`
Extension methods	`Categories`
Rename import	`import java.util.Vector as Vec`
Range	`def range = [a..z]`
Slice	`def slice = list[0..3]`
<< Operator (leftShift)	`list << addMeToList`
Cast operation	`def dog = [name: "Fido", speak: {println "woof"}] as Dog`
GString	`def gString = "Dog's name is ${dog.name}"`

APPENDIX B

Java/Scala[1]

Feature	Java	Scala
Public class	`public class`	`class`
Loops	`for(Type it : c){...}`	`c.foreach {...}`
Lists	`List list = asList(1,2,3);`	`val list = List(1,2,3)`
Maps	`Map m = ...; m.put(x,y);`	`val m = Map(x -> y)`
Function def.	`void method(Type t) {}`	`def method(t: Type) = {}`
Mutable value	`Type t`	`var t: Type`
Immutable value	`final Type t`	`val t: Type`
Null safety	`(x == null ? null : x.y)`	`for (a <- Option(x))` `yield a.y`
Null replacement	`(x == null ? "y" : x)`	`Option(x) getOrElse "y"`
Sort	`Collections.sort(list)`	`list.sort(_ < _)`
Wildcard import	`import java.util.*;`	`import scala.collection._`
Var-args	`(String... args)`	`(args: String*)`
Type parameters	`Class<T>`	`Class[T]`
Concurrency	`Fork/Join, Parallel` `Streams`	`Akka`

---

[1]Version 2 of this cheat sheet.

© Adam L. Davis 2020
A. L. Davis, *Modern Programming Made Easy*,
https://doi.org/10.1007/978-1-4842-5569-8

No Java Analog

Feature	Scala
Default closure arg.	_ (underscore is positionally matched)
Default value	`def method(t:String = "yes")`
Add method to object	use `Trait`
Auto-delegate	use `Trait`
Extension methods	implicit class
Rename import	`import scala.collection.{Vector => Vect}`

Null, Nil, etc.

Type	Description
Null	A `Trait` with one instance, null, similar to Java's null.
Nil	Represents an empty `List` of zero length.
Nothing	A `Trait` that is a subtype of everything. There are no instances of it.
None	None signifies no result. Option has two subclasses: Some and None.
Unit	Type to use on a method that does not return a value.

APPENDIX C

Java/JavaScript[1]

Feature	Java	JavaScript
Public class	`public class`	`function`
Loops	`for(Type it : c){...}`	`c.forEach(function() {...})`
Lists	`List list = asList(1,2,3);`	`var list = [1,2,3]`
Maps	`Map m = ...; m.put(x,y);`	`var m = {x: y}`
Function def.	`void method(Type t) {}`	`function method(t) {}`
Mutable value	`Type t`	`var t`
Immutable value	`final Type t`	`const t`
Null safety	`(x == null ? null : x.y)`	`(x == null ? null : x.y)`
Null replacement	`(x == null ? "y" : x)`	`x ? x : 'y'`
Sort	`Collections.sort(list)`	`list.sort()`
Wildcard import	`import java.util.*;`	N/A
Var-args	`(String... args)`	`()`
Type parameters	`Class<T>`	N/A

---

[1]Version 2 of this cheat sheet.

© Adam L. Davis 2020
A. L. Davis, *Modern Programming Made Easy*,
https://doi.org/10.1007/978-1-4842-5569-8

No Java Analog

Feature	JavaScript
Add method to object	t.method = function() {}
Extension methods	Type.prototype.method = function() {}
Add property	t.name = "Bob"

APPENDIX D

Resources

- Java Tutorials[1]

- Java Docs[2]

- Groovy Docs[3]

- Scala Docs[4]

- Grails Docs[5]

- Play Docs[6]

- Heroku Dev Center[7]

- Oracle Code One (on-demand videos[8])

- StackOverflow[9]

- Free Programming Books[10]

---

[1]https://docs.oracle.com/javase/tutorial/
[2]https://docs.oracle.com/en/java/javase/13/
[3]http://groovy-lang.org/documentation.html
[4]https://docs.scala-lang.org/
[5]http://docs.grails.org/latest/guide/index.html
[6]www.playframework.com/documentation/
[7]https://devcenter.heroku.com/
[8]www.oracle.com/code-one/on-demand.html
[9]https://stackoverflow.com/
[10]https://github.com/EbookFoundation/free-programming-books/blob/master/free-programming-books.md

© Adam L. Davis 2020
A. L. Davis, *Modern Programming Made Easy*,
https://doi.org/10.1007/978-1-4842-5569-8

Free Online Learning

Khan Academy[1] is amazing. If you haven't seen it yet, please take a look. The founder started out by teaching his cousins remotely and putting the videos on YouTube. He then created hundreds of videos, teaching millions of people. Khan Academy encompasses nearly every subject: science, math, finance, history, computer science, and more. The amazing thing is, it's all free!

Contrast this, for example, with the price of higher education in the United States. It's been skyrocketing,[2] owing partly to government-funded student loans and partly to other factors.

Online education is flourishing. Many classes in this space are free or very inexpensive. Coursera[3] allows students to take courses from leading institutions, such as Stanford, Princeton, and Emory University. Online interactive platforms such as Codecademy[4] (free) offer to teach you to program.

The Death of College?

Is there any point in going to college anymore? College offers so many benefits other than the obvious textbook knowledge: learning to work with

---

[1]www.khanacademy.org

[2]https://en.wikipedia.org/wiki/Higher_Education_Price_Index

[3]www.coursera.org

[4]www.codecademy.com/learn

© Adam L. Davis 2020
A. L. Davis, *Modern Programming Made Easy*,
https://doi.org/10.1007/978-1-4842-5569-8

others, the social life, athletics, and accountability (not to mention the prestige associated with a degree). However, it seems like these benefits could be achieved in different, less expensive ways—perhaps not a degree but something like certificates, which could be just as useful.

You've probably been able to simply buy books and teach yourself or learn by doing, so let's not overestimate the potential of online learning. However, with so many alternatives cropping up and the advantages of college being questionable, it's easy to imagine education being less expensive in the future.

Sustainability

Sure that's all great, but are these "schools" sustainable? What is the business model? Well, Khan Academy is a not-for-profit[5] venture, so its future is entirely dependent on the generosity of donors. The other institutions cited are conventional companies. Some offer free samplers, with normal courses requiring tuition. Coursera and its peers will most likely charge only for the certificate, not the actual learning. This is a promising business model.

More Online Resources

The following is a list of various web sites offering the opportunity to learn just about anything:

- *Khan Academy*[6]: Math, Python

- *Codecademy*[7]: JavaScript, HTML/CSS, PHP, Python, Ruby

---

[5]www.khanacademy.org/about

[6]www.khanacademy.org

[7]www.codecademy.com/learn

- *Coursera*[8]: Algorithms, Programming, etc.

- *Pluralsight*[9]: Ruby, Python, JavaScript, HTML/CSS, iOS

- *Udacity*[10]: Everything from "Introduction to Computer Science" to "Applied Cryptography"

- *CodeCombat*[11]: Learn JavaScript through a game

- *EdX*[12]: Free online courses by Harvard, MIT, and more

---

[8]www.coursera.org/courses
[9]www.pluralsight.com
[10]www.udacity.com
[11]https://codecombat.com
[12]www.edx.org/

APPENDIX F

Java

Java[1] was first developed in the 1990s by James Gosling. It borrowed much of its syntax from C and C++ to be more appealing to programmers at the time. Java was owned by Sun Microsystems, which was acquired by Oracle in 2010.

Java is a *statically typed*, *object-oriented* language. "Statically typed" means that every variable and parameter must have a defined type, as opposed to languages such as JavaScript, which are dynamically typed. "Object-oriented" (OO) means that data and functions are grouped into objects (functions are usually referred to as *methods* in OO languages). With the introduction of lambda expressions in Java 8, the Java language better supports the functional style of programming as well.

Java code is compiled to bytecode that runs on a virtual machine (the Java Virtual Machine, JVM). The virtual machine handles garbage collection and allows Java to be compiled once and run on any OS or hardware that has a JVM. This is an advantage over C/C++, which must be compiled directly to machine code and has no automatic garbage collection (the programmer has to allocate and de-allocate memory).

The standard implementation of the JVM is packaged in two different ways: the JRE (Java Runtime Environment) and the JDK (Java Development Kit). The JRE is strictly for running Java as an end user, while the JDK is for developing Java code. The JDK comes with the `javac` command for compiling Java code to bytecode, among other things.

---

[1]Java is a registered trademark of Oracle.

© Adam L. Davis 2020
A. L. Davis, *Modern Programming Made Easy*,
https://doi.org/10.1007/978-1-4842-5569-8

As of this writing, Java is one of the most popular programming languages in use,[2] particularly for server-side web applications.

The Java ecosystem is huge. It's mainly composed of JVMs, libraries, tools, and IDEs. If you'd like to learn more, you could read *Modern Java: Second Edition*[3] which delves more deeply into the ecosystem.

---

[2]www.tiobe.com/tiobe-index//
[3]https://leanpub.com/modernjavasecondedition/

Afterword

If you've gotten this far, congratulations! You probably know a lot more than when you started (I hope). This book ended up being a lot longer than initially planned and, at first, some readers might even think, "Hey! That's not easy!"

It turns out that programming can be challenging and complex. There are many layers to a typical program covering different levels of abstraction, and a whole version control mess if you work on a large team. However, I stand by the title of the book. To me, what really makes something easy is if it's fun or rewarding. If it's not fun or rewarding, even the simplest task, such as doing dishes, seems difficult. However, if something is fun, a person will be inclined to spend hours a day at it, becoming a master through practice over time.

I hope that you have found something fun in this book. If not, please think of an alternative you do find fun or rewarding (sports, music, movies, or something else) and write a program related to it. That is the best way to learn programming.

You can also benefit from looking at open source projects. For example, go to github[1] and search for existing projects in the language of your choice. There are also a lot of resources out there to help people learning how to program. Some are listed in the appendix of this book.

---

[1]https://github.com/

© Adam L. Davis 2020
A. L. Davis, *Modern Programming Made Easy*,
https://doi.org/10.1007/978-1-4842-5569-8

Index

A

Actor design pattern, 66
Application program interface
    (API), 121, 122, 154
Arrays, 23, 24, 27
assertEquals method, 113
Assignment, 10–11
@Autowired, 57

B

Behavior-driven development
    (BDD), 120
Boolean algebra/Boolean logic, 36

C

Cassandra, 170
Chain of responsibility
    pattern, 67
Class and object
    comments, 15
    create new object, 14
    field, properties and
        methods, 12, 13
    Groovy, 13
    Javascript prototype, 14
    Scala, 14

Conditional statement
    Boolean logic, 36
    if, then, else, 33, 34
    looping, 37, 38
    switch, 34

D, E

Design patterns
    actors, 66
    Chain of Responsibility, 67, 68
    DSL
        closures, 63, 64
        definition, 63
        operators, 65
    Facade, 68
    MVC, 61
    observer, 59, 60
Domain-specific language
    (DSL), 63–65, 105, 168
doSomething() method, 37

F

Facade pattern, 68
Functional interface, 73
Functional programming (FP)
    closure, 72
    concat, 77, 78

Printed in the United States
By Bookmasters